the Persian kitchen

My thanks go to all those people in Iran and Germany whose knowledge and helpfulness made it possible for this book to be published.

I would like to extend my particular thanks to the Persian women cooks who made their family recipes available to me. A heartfelt thank you to Florentine Schwabbauer, who inspired the project and provided the wonderful photos that depict modern life in Iran so vibrantly; and, of course, to Peter-Arnold Mumm, who helped me with all the background research and the wording of the text, as well as to Tanja Germann, who expertly proofread my recipes.

Concept: Florentine Schwabbauer, Tanja Germann
Editor: Tanja Germann
Technical advice: Dr. Peter-Arnold Mumm
Illustrated map: Karin Nahr
Proofreader: Petra Tröger
Setting and layout: Wigel, Munich
Jacket design: Caroline Daphne Georgiadis,
Daphne Design

PLEASE NOTE:

Fresh herbs are sold in very different forms, which means that their weight at the time of sale can vary considerably. For the recipes in this book, once all the coarse stems have been removed, you should be left with at least half the quantity of herbs given in the recipe to use in the dish.

DISCLAIMER

Neda Afrashi

the Persian kitchen

home cooking from the Middle East

FOOD PHOTOGRAPHY
Oswald Baumeister

LANDSCAPE PHOTOGRAPHY
Florentine Schwabbauer

MITCHELL BEAZLEY

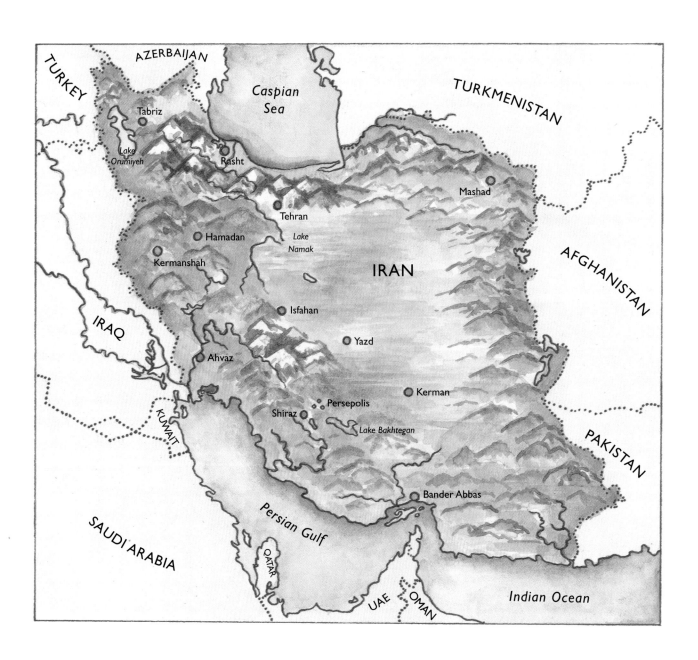

CONTENTS

PERSIAN COOKERY

Persian cookery is still a relatively unknown quantity in Western Europe. A rather outdated impression of Oriental opulence run riot still exists, but not many people know that this old, fairy-tale world actually has its roots in reality, and still lives on in an astonishingly vital way. What most of us grew up with – the concept of the culinary luxury of the Orient, with its exotic variety and bewildering array of spices – came from traditions that ran through Persia herself.

Today, as in the past, Persian cuisine reflects the splendour of the royal courts, the rustic cooking of the villages, and the refined taste of the noble families of the cities. Sampling a *Shirin polo*, a sweet rice dish with pistachios, sultanas, bitter-orange peel and roast chicken, you begin to see why authors once waxed lyrical about the delicacies of the Orient. An *ash-e jo*, on the other hand, a thick barley soup made according to an age-old recipe, will probably stir up memories of country dishes now almost forgotten. With the addition of lamb, dried mint and fresh, aromatic herbs, not to mention special secret ingredients, a simple barley soup is transformed into a delicacy to make even a king's mouth water.

It is no surprise that Europeans have only a hazy idea of Persian cuisine. Even in the 1950s and 1960s, European tourism extended only to the Mediterranean countries. Later, as Europeans ventured further afield, the 1979 Islamic Revolution in particular ensured that their familiarity with the scents of the Orient owed more to *A Thousand and One Nights* than first-hand experience of Iranian food. This gap in our knowledge is something to be regretted.

Left: Work and pleasure – there is a time for everything at the bazaar. The arches in Tabriz date back to the 15th century.

Persian cuisine has more than a little to offer the culinary explorer. It is not simply a halfway house between Indian, Far Eastern, Arabian and Turkish cookery. Unlike Indian cuisine, Persian cooking is very sparing with its seasonings and spice mixtures.

In contrast to the rice of eastern Asia, Persian rice is not sticky, but fluffy and fragrant. Persian cuisine does not share the predilection for hot, spicy foods that is common in many Arab countries, and unlike Turkish cuisine, for example, Persian food is not characterized by Mediterranean influences. Olive oil, potatoes, tomatoes and peppers, introduced only in fairly recent times, are nothing more than a marginal element of traditional Persian cuisine.

HISTORICAL BACKGROUND

Elements from central and southern Asia, as well as Arabian, Caucasian and Mediterranean influences, are nevertheless contained in Persian cuisine. Persia was always a nerve centre of trade between East and West, and since the dawn of history, ownership of the land has always been hotly disputed.

With the immigration of ancient Persian nomadic tribes in the second millennium BC, the central Asian world began to dominate in a Persia that had already long been inhabited. Hellenistic influences then arrived, with Alexander the Great's campaigns in the 4th century BC, moving on to Arabian overtones with the Islamic conquest in the 7th century AD, and returning to Central Asian with the Mongolian conquest in the 13th century.

Later still, the northern Indian world would make its mark. Throughout this time, the Silk Road trade routes led across the steppes and mountain ranges of Persia and, when not using the sea routes, the peoples of South-East Asia, the Near East, the Arabian world, the Caucasus and the Mediterranean all pursued their trade here.

TRADE

Overland travel was organized in caravans. These were
highly armed, well-organized protection forces – the word
caravan is derived from the ancient Persian *kara*, or 'army'
— which traders could join for a consideration. Without
this, the safety of property and life in the desolate desert,
steppe, and mountain regions could not be guaranteed.
The caravans followed fixed routes that had been travelled
for centuries. Handed down from generation to generation
by the caravan leaders, who were often nomadic in origin,
these routes were maintained and extended by the regional
and central rulers, who protected their own interests.
Whenever the central power of the land offered stability,
there was lively traffic along the caravan routes. As far
back as the time of Christ, under Parthian rule, an
extensive network of caravan routes had existed. Even the
11th-century Turkish Tartar conquerors, having destroyed
and laid waste to so many cities and so much farmland,
happily took over Persia's role as a nerve centre of trade,
and the caravan roads were well-maintained under their

rule. The routes again experienced a new lease of life with
the ascendancy of the Safavid dynasty in 1501, after which
the highways and many other aspects of life were systemat-
ically improved.

The stunning city of Rey, today inconspicuously merged
into the south-eastern periphery of Tehran, was for a long
time the centre of all international trade routes. Tehran
itself was only founded in the late 18th century. With
the accession of the Safavid dynasty, the centre of the
caravan network shifted to Isfahan, considered a pearl
among cities. The city of Shiraz also became important,
inter alia, as an international terminal of the wine trade.
Even in ancient times, the trade routes were so extensive
and so well-provided with stopping places (*caravansarai*)
that goods could cover enormous distances. Trade
flourished with India even before the Arabs conquered
Persia in the 7th century. Many of the fruits and raw
products that came originally from India, for example,
were native to Persia before being spread around the world
with the help of the Arabs. These included spices of all

Left: Detail from the Great Mosque in Isfahan.
The tile work covering the inner dome is a masterpiece;
its upkeep has been in the hands of a single family
for centuries.

Below: The salt steppe, which extends over large parts of
the country, is inhospitable to all but a few animal species.

kinds, rice, cane sugar, aubergines (eggplants), many kinds of citrus fruit, and watermelons, whose name in Persian is *hendevaneh*, or 'the Indian one'.

ARISTOCRATIC INFLUENCES

All these fruits and crops were introduced in ancient times. Rice was already known in antiquity from long-distance trade with China and India, and was cultivated early on in Persia, in Gilan and Khuzestan. However, it was an expensive luxury food, and as such for many years played no more than a culinary supporting role. Then, from the 16th century onwards, it became the main cultivated crop. It was the Safavid court chefs who reinvented rice as a focal point of the cuisine, opening new horizons for its domestic cultivation.

It was also under the Safavids that Persian cuisine acquired its specific characteristics. The expansion and refinement of rice cookery and the appropriate sauces was so successful that it even led to rice dishes being exported back into India: the cuisine of the Indian Great Moghuls ('Great Mongols') drew its inspiration from Persian cookery. A distinguishing feature of the north Indian Imperial Moghul cuisine, which also experienced its heyday in the 16th century, is the absorption of Persian (and also Mediterranean) elements into the otherwise fairly strictly

Left: in the high-altitude pastures of the Zagros Mountains
lie the summer quarters of the nomads, who move
in winter to the southwestern slopes.

Hindu Ayurvedic cuisine. The Moghuls loved meat, as
well as the catalogue of refined Persian ingredients that
included yogurt, raisins and dried fruits, Persian herbs,
cardamom, nuts and clarified butter.

PEASANT INFLUENCES

In addition to expanding the culinary arts in the Safavid
court, however, Persian cookery also preserved its earlier
influences. Among the oldest of these is *ash*, the thick
soup made from grain, vegetables and herbs from which
Persian cookery in general actually derives its name
(*ash-pazi*, whose literal meaning is 'thick-soup cooking',
translates as both 'kitchen' and 'cuisine'). Today, the
many age-old regional traditions for growing and
preparing fruit, vegetables, pulses and herbs are still alive
and well throughout Iran. In 1865, Jakob Eduard Polak,
the former personal physician of Naser-od Din Shah, wrote
as follows: '*Ash pas* (meaning "the *ash*-cooker") is the
Persian name for the cook, since the art of the master is
expressed in the appetizing preparation and consistency
of this soup. Gourmands seldom find an *ash* that is
entirely to their taste; special invitations are made based
on artistically prepared *ashes*. Several times a year, the
king had the steward (*hadshib-e dawle*) prepare the *ash*
in the castle courtyard in his presence, and would
sometimes exclaim in a transport of delight: *Adsheb ash est!*
– "It's marvellous!" It was then brought out in large
Chinese bowls, with three unpeeled oranges bobbing
on the surface.'

NOMADIC INFLUENCES

Every bit as ancient as the peasant tradition is the nomadic
culinary tradition of meat and dairy products. As far as
we know, the first Persian immigrants in the second
millennium BC were nomads who lived less from
agriculture than from animal husbandry. One good source

of information is the holy writings of Zoroaster, which
date from around 1000 BC. His ancient Persian *gathas*, or
chants – actually profound religious songs – also give us an
insight into contemporary life. Zoroaster belonged to the
Persian tribes which, after moving to the Persian
highlands from the northeast, had settled in eastern Persia
towards the end of the second millennium BC. It is likely
that they took up agriculture there, as well as continuing
to keep animals as they had always done. Zoroaster's chants
ring time and time again with complaints against
predatory tribes swarming in from the northeast and
slaughtering his people's cattle.

For ancient Persians, cattle were the most important
possession, outranking even sheep and goats. This was also
true of the closely related Vedic Indians, who expressed
their wealth in cattle. Cattle must have played quite a
special role for these Indo-Iranian tribes, both for milk
production, and more importantly as providers of meat
and sacrificial beasts. The whole Zoroastrian livestock-
based economy revolved around the cow. From the Avesta
word for cow (*gaosh*) the Persians derived their word for
meat (*gusht*) and oddly enough their word for sheep
(*gusfand*), too, taken from the Avesta word *gaospeta*,
meaning 'sacred cow'.

RELIGIOUS BACKGROUND

Cattle sacrifice must on occasion have assumed huge
proportions because Zoroaster intervened forcefully against
it, demanding moderation and compassion for the beasts.
His defence of cattle simultaneously acquired the status
of a defence of a well-ordered, civilized way of life, in
contrast to the life of the marauding, cattle-slaughtering
foreign tribes. By extension, this grew into a championing
of a proper world order in general, and a rejection of
evil and deceitful principles. So it was that the ox also
became the mythical first living creature, created by the
great and just god *Ahura Mazda* ('God of Wisdom').
Here, Zoroaster did not go as far in his practical

Above right: Outside Yazd, the present-day centre of Zoroastrianism, you can visit the Towers of Silence. Here, the dead were laid out according to ancient ritual as late as the 1960s.

Below right: The winged sun-disc, symbol of the ancient Persian deity *Ahura Mazda*, is portrayed as a relief in Persepolis.

instructions as the Hindu movement would do later in India, where the cow became totally sacrosanct. Zoroaster raised the cow to be an object of religious esteem, but the sacrifice of cattle and the consumption of beef were permitted, although only if carried out according to exact ritual instructions, and only when the rules of animal husbandry were obeyed to the letter. Precise precepts on the regular duties of animal husbandry were given in the Middle Persian Zoroastrian scripture *Shayest Ne-Shayest* ('Proper and Improper'). 'He who would please *Vahman* (the divine principle of Good Thought) in the world should please the beneficent beast. He shall keep it in a pleasant, warm place; in summer, he shall store up straw and grain, so that it need not spend the winter in the fields. He shall not separate the cow from its young, nor the young from its mother's milk.'

When an ox was sacrificed, a feast was always held for the sacrificing community, and not just a religious one. Unlike today, sacrifice then meant eating well, rather than going without. A portion of the meat would certainly have been set aside for the god, but this was symbolic only: the portion would later have been eaten by the sacrificers themselves. In Zoroastrianism, many different animals were permitted to be used sacrificially, including goats, sheep, oxen, asses, wild asses, ibex, gazelles, and even pigs.

With the Arab conquest of Persia and the triumph of Islam, the consumption of pork was well and truly over. To this day, pork is taboo, regardless of whether the household is religious or not. Pork simply seems to have no appeal for the Persian palate.

MEDICAL BACKGROUND

A special feature of Persian cookery is its medicinal aspects. Ingredients are usually classified as warm, cold, damp or dry. Sometimes entire dishes are composed with these qualities in mind. Occasionally, the constitution

and disposition of the guest are also taken into account, with the meal meant to produce greater inner harmony in the diner. Sometimes incorrectly seen as a legacy of Zoroaster, this approach can actually be traced back to the medicine practised in ancient Greece, whose famous proponents were Hippocrates, Dioscurides and Galen. It had probably begun to be accepted in Persia from the time of Alexander the Great, and although the country was then primarily under Muslim rule, it was faithfully translated and applied by Arab and Arabic-writing Persian scholars. Great scholars such as Ibn Sina (known to the West as Avicenna, AD 980–1037), the Prince of All Sciences, perpetuated and extended this area of medical understanding.

Al-Biruni (AD 973–1048) wrote in his pharmacopoeia that 'each individual nation has achieved something outstanding in some science or practical activity or other. Among them, before the introduction of Christianity, the Greeks distinguished themselves by particularly painstaking research, and they took what they did to a high level – indeed, almost to perfection. Had Dioscurides lived in our country and applied his zeal to the knowledge of what our mountains and steppes have to offer, all of their herbs would have been transformed into medicaments, and what can be collected from them, thanks to his experience, would have become a remedy.'

A basic concept of Greek–Arab–Persian medicine was that of the four elementary components of the human organism: the warm, cold, damp and dry components. These four components made up the four bodily humours: blood, phlegm, yellow bile and black bile. Blood was warm and damp; phlegm cold and damp; yellow bile was warm and dry; black bile cold and dry. Black bile, incidentally, was an invention of convenience, as in reality it exists neither in healthy nor sick organisms. As these schools of medical thought perceived it, the bodily humours, expanded thus into a 'system', constituting a proper structure that had to be in balance, or the individual in question would become ill. Here, the same mixture ratio was not deemed equally effective for each individual; the different dispositions of the various hu-

man natures and stages of life were all taken into account.

Another critically important notion was that these natural differences were fundamentally nothing more than different mixture ratios of blood, phlegm, yellow bile, and black bile. From this arose the famous theory of the four human temperaments: phlegmatic, melancholic, sanguine, and choleric, each brought about by a natural predominance of phlegm (phlegmatic, cold and damp), black bile (melancholic, cold and dry), blood (sanguine, warm and damp) or yellow bile (choleric, warm and dry).

The stages of human life were also related to the theory of humours: childhood was considered to be sanguine, youth (puberty) choleric, adulthood melancholic, and old age phlegmatic. Accordingly, the various temperaments as well as the stages of life had their own specific balance of bodily fluids. A disturbance in this balance meant illness.

The reproduction of bodily fluids happens naturally via eating and drinking, and the theory of humours was therefore extended to food and drink. Dietetics – the science of the systematic contribution of nutrition to physical health – was thus born. All foods were to be classified according to the four categories of warm, cold, dry and damp, and each individual should consume different foods, depending on temperament and stage of life. This theory was accepted completely by Persian and Arab medicine, then further developed and widely popularized. Ibn Sina (Avicenna) taught that the system of the four bodily humours depended on the composition of foods and their degree of digestibility. The most highly digestible foods were transformed into blood (warm and damp), somewhat less digestible ones to phlegm (cold and damp), raw and coarse foods to yellow bile (warm and dry) and poorly digestible-to-indigestible foods to black bile (cold and dry).

The division of foods according to these categories is a science in itself. It can frequently vary from region to region and even from family to family, and one and the same individual is even reported as abruptly changing his viewpoint over the course of two hours. Regardless of this, the subject is a popular one for debate. J. E. Polak, the court physician mentioned on page 11, held that it sometimes went too far: 'In all classes of the population, even with the rough warriors of Afghanistan, Sistan, Turkistan and Chiwa, these ideas have been adopted as shibboleths. The patient comes to the doctor already armed with a diagnosis relating to heat or damp, demanding nothing but a "corresponding remedy".

With everything that the Persian consumes, he ponders beforehand whether it will engender heat or cold, damp or dryness in the body, and during the mealtimes of the Great, and in particular at the table of the Shah, almost the entire conversation would revolve around these catchwords.'

Many of the characterizations are easy to understand. That pepper and caraway or cumin are warm and dry, and cucumbers are cold and damp is not difficult to grasp. One needs a little more intuition, though, to understand lamb, honey, mint and black tea as 'warm', and beef, melon, peaches and green tea as quite the opposite: 'cold'.

Even with all the inconsistencies, however, it would not be an entirely pointless exercise to think long and hard about the overall composition of the meal in terms of this elementary theory. It should also be remembered that these tenets became very believable, and were disseminated far beyond the borders of Persia, being found both in Indian Ayurvedic cooking and in the 12th-century writings of the German mystic and visionary Hildegard von Bingen. With this in mind, wherever the medicinal properties and uses for certain foods are known, these have been described in the Ingredients A to Z (*see* Appendix, pages 175–185).

THE CHARACTER OF THE INGREDIENTS

Present-day Persian cuisine encompasses all these different regional and foreign, nomadic and peasant, aristocratic and everyday, religious and medical influences. Despite their very diverse origins, the various popular and courtly traditions have converged over the last few centuries; indeed, in the last few decades they have become a coherent national cuisine.

Even the old traditions seem to have a greater cohesion. The small number of older-style cookery books that have survived in written form, written by professionals for professionals and dating back to the Safavid and Qajar eras, are referred to alongside the countless oral traditions within families, handed down from one generation to the next, which still have plenty of currency even today. Since the beginning of the 20th century, however, the educated city-dwellers have helped to increase the scope of Persian cookery by going out and gathering recipes in order to pass them on in writing.

Because of this, the social differentials once present in Persian cookery have also tended to level out. The aristocratic Safavid cuisine has become universal and simplified, while the simplest peasant elements such as fresh flatbread have become indispensable accompaniments of the Persian meal in even the finest restaurants. Recipes no longer make the basic distinction between rich and poor, and, while the quality and quantity of the raw ingredients will vary, the more expensive ingredients such as meat are now found in both everyday and special-occasion cuisine.

MEAT

Although meat has always been an indicator of wealth, the special nature of *khoresh*, *polo* and *ash* means that meat does not predominate over all the other ingredients. For Europeans – at least for those who have not gone over to vegetarianism – meat is the main focus of the meal, with vegetables, rice or pasta usually seen as side dishes. In Persian cookery, the traditional focus is different; the main component is well-prepared rice, together with a painstakingly planned vegetable recipe, and often complemented with fruit, nuts or herbs. Finally, a few pieces of meat will be added, to round everything off. This is even the case with the choicest of dishes. In *khoresh*, *polo* and *ash*, meat is just one ingredient among many, although this does not mean that meat is unimportant, as only a very few dishes are totally vegetarian. In most dishes, the meat is what rounds out the overall taste, and if you try making a recipe leaving out the meat, the difference is very noticeable: *kalam polo* without the beef, for example, tastes rather insipid.

There are, of course, other dishes in which meat plays the dominant part: *kabab* (grilled meat on a spit or skewer) and *beryani* (whole spit-roasted mutton, goats and oxen) are two such examples. Both have a very old tradition. Whole oxen were roasted at the festive banquets of the ancient Persian royal dynasties and the extravagance of these banquets was legendary. A report on the subject by the Greek–Egyptian writer Athenaeus has survived: 'Every day a thousand beasts are slaughtered for the king, including horses, camels, oxen, asses, stags, and various smaller animals; and many birds are eaten, including Arabian ostriches, geese and chickens. Each of the King's guests is served moderate portions thereof, but each may take home with him whatever he leaves at the table. Most of the meat and other dishes are distributed to the royal guard and to the armed troops, for whom the King must provide.'

The Persians also had a liking for grilled or broiled meats. In the first volume of the *Histories*, the ancient Greek historian Herodotus reports that wealthy Persians thought it '... appropriate to put on a more lavish meal on their birthdays than on other days: the wealthy among them lay on an ox, a horse, a camel and an ass, which are roasted whole in the oven; the poor among them serve smaller animals.' This custom endured for many centuries. From

17th-century Isfahan, the Eastern traveller Jean-Baptiste Tavernier reported on grill-houses in which a whole sheep hung in an oven over a large pan of rice, into which the fat dripped. Isfahan still harbours the occasional similar grill-house even today.

The more manageable method of grilling is the *kebab*, made with tender sliced or ground meat threaded onto skewers. Today, lamb, mutton and beef are used almost exclusively, with goat meat less frequently on the menu. The sheep is the most important source of meat in Iran, and sheep numbered 35 million there in the mid-1980s. The number of goats, which of course can be grazed on very infertile soils, cannot be far behind. Even nowadays, stock-breeding is still to a large extent in the hands of the nomads. If you are travelling in Iran in the spring or autumn, wherever you go you will come across small knots of nomads in the process of moving from winter to summer pastures, or vice versa. In the province of Fars, for example, it is the Qashqai or the Loren who are to be seen by the roadside or on the horizon, scattered about

in many small groups with their huge herds of small domestic beasts. Usually, they have to make do with meagre soils, the better ones being unavailable to them. It is precisely this impoverished soil, however, that has provided an enduring livelihood for the nomads. Unsuitable for agricultural use, the land has always yielded enough for keeping sheep and goats, and today there are still a considerable number of sheep- and goat-rearing nomads. Things are different in the fertile Caspian regions, and particularly in Gilan, where the sedentary stock-breeder usually keeps fairly large herds of animals, and has both social prestige and richer soil on his side.

Even in these regions, animal husbandry is carried out in style and over an extensive territory, as is the stock-breeding of the nomads, albeit on a smaller scale. The animals are pastured on open fields, grazing on whatever grows there, and the European practice of intensive animal rearing using animal-based fodder, growth hormones and antibiotics is still, mercifully, unknown in Iran.

The tales from *A Thousand and One Nights*
are known to have originated in many
different lands – from Arabia, Turkey,
Israel, India, China and, not least,
from Persia. Even the main
character Sheherazade (from
shehr-zadeh 'the high-born')
has a Persian name. The stories are
ancient folk-tales, and the roots of this compilation
of tales made into an elaborately interwoven
framework date back at least one thousand years.
Leaving this aside, there still exists in Iran today an
unbroken oral storytelling tradition drawn from
a profusion of additional material. Just a few
decades ago, researchers in Iran collected and
recorded these folk-tales much as the Brothers Grimm
had done in Germany in their time: tales of magic
and adventure, love stories, anecdotes about mischief
and cunning, parables, sagas and legends.
The following is a typical Persian picaresque tale.

THE SLY GOLDSMITH

Once upon a time in a city there lived a Goldsmith who was wise to the ways of the world, and nobody's fool. His wife, however, was lazy and stupid. One day he gave her some cotton to spin into yarn. 'Oh, I don't feel like spinning just now' she said. 'And just when will you feel like it?' 'God only knows.' Days later, as the man was sleeping, his wife was taking a bath. Suddenly she began screaming at the top of her voice, so that the Goldsmith started awake and came running. 'What is going on?' he asked, and was vexed to see her sitting peacefully in the tub. 'Oh, nothing, really. I just this moment felt like spinning!' This made the Goldsmith's blood boil, and he beat his capricious wife and commanded her to finish spinning the yarn by that very evening, or else her marriage to him would be at an end. When he came home that evening, his first question was about the yarn. 'Oh, the urge to spin soon passed, so I put the yarn outside by the moat, so that the dear frogs would spin it.' Saying this, she went outside, picked up a hefty stone and placed it in the hand of her flabbergasted husband: 'There is your yarn!' This was too much for the afflicted man, and that very same hour he chased her from his house.

The wife wandered for many hours, and finally, in the depths of the night, sat down on a stone. Along came a cat. 'Good day, Aunt Cat! Did my husband send you? Go and tell him I shall not be coming back!' The cat went off, the moon moved slowly on its way, and the woman became tired and hungry. Then a she-ass came along. 'Good day, Aunt She-Ass! Did my husband send you? Go and tell him I shall not be coming back!' The ass went off, the moon became paler and moved slowly on its way, and fear crept into the woman. Along came a camel with a heavy load, her bell jingling merrily through the vanishing night. 'Good day, Aunt Long-Neck! Surely my husband must have sent you! Very well then, I'll patch things up with him!' Saying this, she mounted the camel and rode home.

The Goldsmith was less than pleased, but he consoled himself with the thought that a camel was certainly worth something. And as he opened the saddlebags, he saw that they contained a large quantity of pure gold. Straight away he took the gold and dragged it piece by piece into his cellar. The camel, however, he decided to slaughter.

The next day, the Shah's messengers roamed the streets, announcing that the Shah's favourite camel had gone astray while carrying a huge quantity of gold, and that whoever returned it would be handsomely rewarded. Curious, the dim-witted woman appeared at the door, and one of the messengers asked her in jest: 'Have you seen the Shah's camel?' 'A camel? Yes, of course! Yesterday, a stray camel brought me home. But whether or not it belongs to the Shah, I really do not know.' That evening, the messengers returned empty-handed to the Shah, and could only report on the simple woman and her story about the camel. 'Hmm,' thought the Shah to himself, 'that is an odd sort of camel story.' So he had the Goldsmith brought before him.

The truth soon came to light. 'You stole my money and killed my camel, so you've earned death twice over. But since you're a Goldsmith, I'll set you a task that may help you to save your skin. Use the gold to make a statue of me – and make it incomparably handsome, so that people in years to come will see how splendid I was!'

The Goldsmith did not wait to be told twice, and set to work without delay. But as he was working, it struck him that so large was the amount of gold that surely no one would notice if he diverted just a tiny bit. The next day the same idea occurred to him again, and so it went on. Finally, the statue was finished, and it really was incomparably handsome. The Shah was delighted, but as he contemplated the statue it struck him as being a little on the small side, so he commanded his servants and ministers to weigh the statue. The courtiers hurried off zealously, but came back distraught, for they could find no scales of sufficient size – not in the palace, nor in the city, nor in the entire land. No one had any idea how such a weight could be weighed, and the King became more and more impatient.

It soon dawned on the Minister that the only one who could solve the problem was probably the Goldsmith himself, who would never voluntarily betray what he knew. The Minister therefore called the dim-witted woman before him, and promised her a rich reward and his very own son's hand in marriage if she managed to prise the secret from her husband.

That evening, the wife spoke to the Goldsmith: 'And how are you, my dear husband?' The husband, long unaccustomed to such affability, countered, 'What in the name of…?' 'Oh, dear Husband, I'm simply dying to know the best way to weigh the statue of the King.' 'What in God's name do you want to know that for?' 'Oh, I'm just curious.' The Goldsmith really did not know what to make of this sudden inquisitiveness, and because he could not imagine that there was anything sinister behind it, he answered obligingly: 'It's not difficult, really. Put the statue in a boat and draw a line on the outside where the water comes up to. Then take the statue out again and fill the boat up with stones that you have previously weighed. Stop when it has sunk again to exactly the same level.'

The woman told this to the Minister, the experiment was performed, and it was revealed that one-quarter of the gold was missing. Now the Shah became truly angry. The Goldsmith was arrested a second time and dragged off to a tall minaret. There he was immured without bread or water, and languished for days and nights, his health and hope gradually fading. At last one day he saw his wife approaching the tower, and she shouted up to him: 'I see you are still alive, but I do not want to continue with our marriage. The Minister has promised me his son, so I've come to fetch the divorce certificate from you!' The Goldsmith rejoiced heartily and said: 'You're right, dear woman. For this purpose, however, you will have to come up to me, since I cannot come down to you. This is the way to do it: catch an ant and tie a thread to its back leg. If you rub some fat on the ant's nose, the ant will follow the smell of the fat and climb up to me. Once it has reached the top and I have the thread in my hand, tie a string to the bottom end of the thread. Once I have the string in my hand, tie a rope to the string, and I'll pull you up with the rope!'

All this was no sooner said than done, and the dim-witted woman was soon standing next to her husband, who greeted her with these words: 'Well done. But it occurs to me that we need a judge for the divorce. I will climb down

this rope and fetch a judge. You wait here for me!' Saying this, he climbed down – and immediately disappeared among the warren of houses in the city.

Meanwhile, the Shah had taken quite a liking to the masterly statue, and gradually regretted so lightly abandoning its artist to his death. He therefore sent his people to free the Goldsmith. How they gaped, though, when they found no one but the Goldsmith's dim-witted wife in the minaret! The Shah, in fact, couldn't suppress a smile, and thought to himself: 'Once again, we'll need to use cunning to catch the Goldsmith.' So he commanded that each family in the city be given a sheep from his herd to tend and feed for twenty days, with the proviso that the sheep had to weigh exactly as much at the end as at the outset – not less, but not one ounce more; and whoever did not comply with this commandment would be severely punished.

Thus it happened, and the man who had given the Goldsmith shelter also received one of the royal sheep. He was very unhappy, and complained bitterly to the Goldsmith about the impossible task. The latter, however, just laughed and said: 'That's not so hard. Go and borrow a wolf. Feed the sheep during the day like one of your own. At night, though, put the wolf in the vicinity of the royal sheep, which will be so afraid it will lose by night the weight that it gained during the day.'

So it was, and as the royal sheep were gathered in after twenty days, what the Shah had expected had come to pass – namely, that all the sheep had either put on or lost weight, except for one, which weighed exactly the same as it had twenty days earlier. The Shah was then able to work out exactly where to find the Goldsmith, and had the latter brought before him for the third time.

And the Shah said: 'We need people in our land who can find a way out of any fix, so henceforth, you will be my right-hand Vizier. However, since I've forgiven you for your misdemeanours, you shall forgive your wife for hers!'

And thus it came to pass.

Retold according to L. Ehlers, 'Persische Märchen und Schwänke' ('Persian Fairy Tales and Comic Tales'), Vienna (Berger) 1961. With the kind permission of the publishers.

Meat still tastes as many people remember it tasted when they were young. Any European wishing to cook Persian-style would be advised to purchase their meat from an organic butcher's shop. At the very least, choose your butcher carefully and make sure you are sold meat of a good quality. The less that spices are used to mask its taste, the more the flavour of the meat shines through — and Persian cooking is sparing with spices.

SPICES

Persian food is very mild. Hot spices are unknown in Persian cuisine, except for black pepper, which is only ever used in moderation. Saffron and turmeric, on the other hand, are used to season almost every dish, and cinnamon is also frequently added. On the whole, however, Persian food remains as unfussy and true to the taste of its actual ingredients as possible. Persian cooking is not a 'cuisine for cheats', and never uses spicy, creamy sauces to camouflage a lack of freshness or inherent flavour. Tasty meat, fragrant rice, intensely tart barberries and limes, sweet, juicy dates and aromatic herbs do not require heavy spicing, and long cooking gives the ingredients a chance to meld to perfection. For this reason, Persian cooking has developed an unmistakeable taste all of its own.

VEGETABLES, FRUIT AND GRAINS

Thanks in part to Nature's generosity, Persian cooking has no need of excessive spicing, as the predominantly dry climate and many sun-drenched days naturally impart an intense aroma and strong flavour to the raw ingredients. This allows the vegetable component to play a starring role in Persian cuisine. In addition, the enormous climatic differences between the various regions of Iran have led to a rich variety of plant crops. The Caspian regions in the north offer a humid, Mediterranean-type climate.

In Iran's most important agricultural region of Gilan, wheat, barley, rice, tobacco, citrus and other fruits, and many varieties of vegetable all flourish. Tea was also traditionally cultivated here, although in recent times this crop has fallen victim to international competition. Tobacco, rice, cotton and sugar beets all flourish in the high steppes of Azerbaijan (which, although semi-arid, have enough rainfall to sustain some crops) and in some of the extensive high plateaux of the Zagros Mountains.

Extensive agriculture also occurs in the inland area between the Alborz and Zagros massifs. In Khuzestan, Bushehr and Hormozgan on the Persian Gulf, the climate is tropical and humid, with summer temperatures that easily reach 40° C in the shade, and high atmospheric humidity. Tropical fruits such as bananas, mangoes and many others grow here, and dates, as well as sugar cane, are abundant. Vast quantities of herbs are cultivated everywhere, from the hot regions to the cold, and from the humid areas to the semi-arid.

Only the two large desert regions in the east and south-east will allow no vegetation of any consequence to grow: the desert of the dry salt seas known as *Dasht-e Kavir* and the even more hostile desert of *Dasht-e Lut*, possibly named after the biblical Lot, but perhaps simply meaning 'empty plain'.

In addition to this major division into climate zones, there are also enormous climatic differences within much smaller areas, sometimes even in adjacent valleys. This is especially true in the region containing the extensive Zagros mountain range. Persia is a land of contrasts both geographically and climatically. Commenting on this phenomenon, the contemporary historian Richard Frye observed that apple or peach trees grow in narrow, mountain valleys, while at no great distance, date-palms or orange trees flourish at oases in the central desert. An earthen wall may be the only thing separating desolate sand and bare rock from a colourful, fragrant garden, and a tough, hardy caravan driver from the cosseted inhabitant of such a private paradise.

FATS AND OILS

What we call 'fast food' can probably be summed up by the words 'hot' and 'greasy'. Persian cooking is the complete opposite of this: it is slow, and uses comparatively little fat. However, it was not always thus. In the past, the fat on the *khoresh* often swam a centimetre deep and the fat-soaked rice from the *beryani* grill could leave you feeling you had eaten enough in one sitting to last for a week. Today, though, all this has changed, even down to the types of fat used. In the past, only mutton- or beef-suet or clarified butter were used in Persian cuisine.

Nowadays, vegetable oils can be imported. Sesame oil, which had been known for a long time, was only used in baking. Olive oil had historically been used only in the northern regions of the country, and olive trees have been grown in the Caspian region for many centuries. However, the intense smell of olive oil, which is nowadays generally perceived as enticing by Europeans accustomed to Mediterranean food, actually seems rather unpleasant to many Persians.

Today's Persians cook with clarified butter and a variety of vegetable oils.

DAIRY PRODUCTS

Persian dairy products are also by nature low in fat.
Yogurt is consumed in large quantities with the main
hot meal, or skimmed and then drunk mixed with water –
a beverage known as *dugh*. The fact that yogurt is
so popular compared to other dairy products may have
something to do with its superior keeping qualities.

Another product made from yogurt is *kashk*; this consists
of skimmed, salted and drained sheep's-milk yogurt.
It is used as a seasoning or, thinned down with water
and boiled, as a sauce to accompany many stews and
other dishes.

With the exception of yogurt, the consumption of dairy
products is not nearly so common in Persia as in Europe.
Cheese in particular plays no more than a very minor role.
The native cheese (*panir*) boasts only a few varieties and
is produced in small quantities, often for home
consumption only. It is not used for cooking or melting,
but rather eaten with bread and herbs as an appetizer, or
even as a meal in itself. The most famous type of cheese is
Lighvan cheese (*panir-e Lighvan*), produced in Tabriz, in
East Azerbaijan province.

SLOW FOOD

Preparing a Persian meal requires a great deal of patience,
at least if one is following the traditional recipes. These
call for cooking over a small flame for hours – a relic of an
earlier social era, when women still stayed at home and
tended to the household. Persian food is genuine 'slow
food'; its preparation takes time, and people also take their
time when eating.

Today, progress has arrived even in Iran, at least in the
cities. Most women now work outside the home, and
seldom find the time to spend hours over a hot stove.
This has meant a change in kitchen equipment; instead

of the simple, large pans that simmered over the fire for
hours at a time, electrical equipment, pressure cookers
and non-stick saucepans are now in widespread use,
helping cooks to prepare meals with a minimum of
effort and in a reasonable amount of time. A pressure
cooker, for example, is a great help when pulses require
pre-cooking.

Persian cooking, despite long preparation times, is
far from tedious, with just a few simple principles and
rules that are easy to follow. Rice takes a good 1 1/2 hours
to cook, and this must be taken into account if you
want to serve it as an accompaniment. Once rice has
been prepared, it will steam away unattended quite
happily over a low heat. The same is true for many
sauces; while they are simmering, other chores can easily
be performed.

TABLE MANNERS AND HOSPITALITY

Anyone who has travelled in Iran will be familiar with
the openness and sociable nature of the Persian people.
And anyone lucky enough to have been entertained by a
Persian family knows that the Persian reputation for
hospitality is well-deserved, and will have enduring
memories of the occasion. It begins with the reception,
which gives the guest the feeling not only of being
welcome, but almost of being long-awaited. Hosts bend
over backwards to ensure that the guest has a pleasant stay
in their home, as well as organizing excursions, further
contacts and attendance at cultural events. The guest is
constantly pampered, and even if the hosts have to put
up with inconveniences in the line of duty, one has the
impression that they are not averse to doing so.

Especially important, of course, is an invitation to a meal,
the way to which is paved by an in-depth chat with the
host. In contrast to our short, terse European opening
gambits, Persians are masters in the art of spinning out a
simple 'hello' and an enquiry after your health, plus all

the relevant constructive answers, into a tapestry of sparkling conversation that can last a good ten minutes. In the meantime, everyone gradually moves towards the seating, making themselves as comfortable as the situation allows. The food then begins to arrive: almonds, fresh and dried pistachios, hazelnuts, fresh and dried walnuts, dried mulberries, sultanas, figs, dates, candied orange peel, fresh fruit, sunflower seeds, melon seeds, peanuts, pastries, confectionery and glazed flaked almonds. Diners lean over the bowls and dishes, eating and chatting in a leisurely way.

Finally, everyone is called to the dinner table. This is the housewife's moment of triumph. Food is brought in – more and more of it, until not an inch of spare space remains on the table beyond the small empty spaces between the crush of platters, plates and bowls. The guest is seated in the best spot, and it sometimes happens that there are not enough seats. The housewife will then hover in the background and oversee the course of the meal. This consists not only of the guest consuming with great relish the delicacies that are placed before him, but also involves the hostess being at pains to ensure that at no point does the guest want for anything.

The hostess takes these duties very seriously. She is not content merely to encourage the guest to take a second helping once his plate is empty: that would be leaving things too long, since the guest might be avoiding polishing off his food merely out of politeness so as not to make his host feel compelled to offer him more. The clever housewife therefore takes precautions, and as soon as the guest has heaped his plate and raised the first forkful to his mouth in pleasurable anticipation, she will begin to lament his lack of appetite, and ask what she might have done wrong, assuring him that the food is good, and fresh, and the guest must have every confidence. It is then the guest's job to express his contentment with a full mouth, reassuring his hostess that he has seldom eaten anything more delicious and that it is his intention to help himself to all the dishes placed before him as far as he is able, going beyond the mere satisfaction of his hunger. This will

not be difficult, as, in all probability, this will actually be the case. Finally, however, even the most hedonistic guest feels full, and is faced with the well-known problem of whether to leave a scrap or two on his plate for the sake of politeness. If he finishes off every last mouthful, his hostess may think he is still hungry – if he leaves anything, there's an implication that he has not actually enjoyed the food. This is a problem whichever way you look at it, so guests are advised just to do whatever seems best in the circumstances, as when all is said and done, this is what the host wants, too! These insoluble 'problems' happen so often in some Eastern cultures that people have become accustomed to not seeing them as in any way problematic.

So much for Persian hospitality. Politeness also has a name, *ta'arof*, which translates most easily as 'courtesy ritual'. Persian life is full of rituals, which, while being practised among Persians themselves, can also naturally be extended towards foreign visitors. The rules must be known and understood, however. Some German friends of mine were once walking through the city on a hot, summery day, and stopped for a drink at one of the many refreshment stalls that sold *ab-e miveh*, freshly squeezed fruit and vegetable juice. They ordered two tumblers of carrot juice. Persian carrots are sweet, and their juice does not conjure up the idea of healthy food. My friends were both pleasantly surprised, and a cheerful atmosphere reigned at the stall. The stallholder naturally went on to say 'The juice is on the house', and my friends insisted back 'No, no, of course we'll pay.' Again the man insisted on treating them, until my friends, flustered and feeling both uneasy and lucky at the same time, walked away. They had hardly gone 30 paces when the juice vendor ran after them, asking where his money was...

This is another form of Persian hospitality. Those who do not understand it run the risk of crashing around like a bull in the china shop of courtesy – perhaps even thinking that they are being duped. One minute it's on the house, the next it's not! But *ta'arof* has nothing to do with a swindle. It is a ritual, which – when played out in the correct way by the participants – is often simply enjoyable, with both parties moving with innocent artfulness through this china shop of communication, holding first one, then another figure of courtesy up to be inspected. It is all just an elaborate game.

The custom of honouring the foreigner as a guest certainly has its roots in history. In the days when journeys took a long time and news was passed on slowly, piecemeal and by word of mouth, a guest was an extremely important person. Wherever it was important to find out the news from the outside, the guest was the messenger – or at the very least, the bearer of messages. It was in this way that a

generally rather cosmopolitan attitude developed, and even those who had no way of drawing any actual profit from their guest would still enjoy the entertainment brought by the stranger's stories and gifts, or even, on occasion, by his peculiar or blundering behaviour.

This tended to happen if an outsider with no knowledge of national customs came on the scene. Professor J. E. Polak commented on this phenomenon: 'Should a European happen along at the beginning of the meal, the Persian is thrown into a quandary, for decency forbids turning him away, but inviting him to sit down is fraught with difficulty, since foods touched by an Unbeliever are

deemed to be unclean. Nevertheless, he, too, is invited to sit down. A foreigner in the know will refuse the invitation with the excuse that he has already eaten. If he does take a seat, however, the clever Persian will know how to serve him so that, under the guise of special attentiveness, his food is kept quite separate. The host does this by allocating the especially fine bowls and drinks to the guest, and by dipping into the ragouts and serving him a generous portion with his own hand. The European will soon find himself completely surrounded by food, which the others present do not touch on the pretext that the host intends it especially for him.

Left and above: Without irrigation, the land cannot be cultivated in the south. Here, village women work together to till the land.

Following pages: The small, pink Nasir ol-Molk Mosque in Shiraz is impressive with its splendid painted tiles, distinguished by an unusually dark shade of blue.

Anyone who is unfamiliar with Persian customs is likely to feel genuinely flattered by this, whereas it is actually just a way out of a dilemma, and the other diners will often make pointed comments afterwards about the simplicity of the guest who fancied himself to be "honoured".'

This problem has lost its urgency, however, ever since people began to use a spoon and fork (knives are only rarely needed when eating Persian cooking) and to eat from their own plates where they would once be dipping into a communal bowl with their hand or a piece of bread. At a more general level, too, the superstitious concern about the unclean nature of the unbeliever has largely vanished.

What clearly remains unchanged is the pleasure that people take in offering hospitality, and it is universally true that the length and breadth of the country, people like to take their time, which is there for chatting, eating and enjoying themselves.

SIDE DISHES

BORANI, DOLMEH, KUKU AND TORSHI

The concept of a series of courses served in a fixed sequence according to the French model does not exist in Persian cookery. There is no menu, but dishes gradually accumulate on the table, which becomes more and more seductive as it fills up.

Having said that, the food definitely arrives in a certain order, and everything is planned around the rice. From the point of view of the timing of the meal, the rice, and everything directly related to it – in other words, the *khoresh* (similar in consistency to an Indian curry) or the *kebab* (meat) – is both the central point and the climax of the meal. Everything savoury that is not directly related to the rice is often served beforehand, and is not cleared away until the rice is finished.

Depending on the intended variety and lavishness of the meal, a whole range of very different dishes are served at the early stage of the meal: things that can be spooned up with a piece of flatbread, such as a variety of yogurt preparations, purées or dips; and food that can be held in the hand, all preceded by a basket of various fresh herbs (*sabzi*) such as flatleaf parsley, chives, dill, fresh mint, basil, coriander and perhaps some crunchy radishes. The herbs are simply trimmed and washed (and allowed to dry before serving), and are eaten without any dressing. Raw onions are often included with the fresh herbs, having been scalded and then dipped in cold water to reduce their strong taste. Alternatively, a quartered onion is soaked for a few minutes in cold water, which achieves the same effect, or a milder type of onion can be cut into rings, wedges or smaller pieces.

Titbits such as omelet slices or stuffed peppers, marinated olives and salads are also often served at the beginning of a meal. It is recommended that you think carefully about the quantities of ingredients given in the recipes and reduce them if necessary, if you are not serving the dish as a main course, or if several such dishes are being served, as Iranian quantities are always on the generous side!

The items that are always brought to the table first are the basket of fresh herbs, the little bowl of raw onions, a bowl of yogurt, and fresh, fragrant bread, along with a jug of clear, cold water.

There is no pressure to finish these off before the main dish is brought in; they are there to snack on and are not cleared away. Shortly afterwards, *borani* (yogurt salads or dips), purées, *kuku* (omelets) or *dolmeh* (stuffed vine-leaves or vegetables) begin to arrive, along with perhaps a tomato and cucumber salad (*salad-e shirazi*) or a chicken salad (*salad-e olivieh*). *Torshi* (sour pickled fruit and vegetables) is often passed around at this point, but it does not have to be eaten right away. Some people like to eat *torshi* on its own, while others prefer it as a condiment with the rice.

If the cook has been conscientious and has provided a wide variety of dishes, the diners are now faced with the dilemma of wanting to try everything, while still keeping enough room for the rice course. This is an inevitable dilemma, and one to which there is no easy answer. The wise gourmand should simply ignore all siren calls of abstinence. Relax and enjoy!

HALIM BADEMJAN
AUBERGINE (EGGPLANT) PURÉE

SERVES 4–6 AS A MAIN COURSE,
8–10 AS AN APPETIZER

5–6 small aubergines (eggplants), approx 600g/1lb 5oz

salt

3 onions

oil

500g (1lb 2oz) shoulder of lamb (with bone)

4–5 tablespoons *kashk*, or sour cream

175g (6oz) *adas*, black caviar lentils

3–4 garlic cloves, coarsely chopped

5–6 tablespoons dried mint

1/4 teaspoon saffron, ground

10 walnut halves, finely chopped

1 Peel the aubergines and cut them lengthwise into thick slices. Place side by side on paper towel and sprinkle with salt. Leave for about 2 hours – the longer you leave them, the less oil they will absorb when fried.

2 Quarter one of the onions. Heat some oil in a large pan and fry the onion pieces until golden brown. Add the lamb and brown slightly on all sides. Pour in 1.5 litres (55fl oz) water, cover, and simmer gently for 2 hours.

3 If using the *kashk*, decant it from its jar into a small pot. Add 250ml (9fl oz) water, and cook uncovered over a low-to-medium heat for 20 minutes, stirring frequently. Cover and set aside.

4 Rinse and sort through the lentils, then stir in with the meat. Simmer the mixture for about 1 hour, adding extra water if necessary.

5 Pat the aubergines dry. Pour oil to a depth of about 1cm (1/2-inch) into a non-stick pan over a moderate heat. Fry the aubergines in batches until they are golden brown on both sides.

6 Finely chop the remaining 2 onions. Heat some oil in a small pan and fry the onions until golden brown, then set aside.

7 Lift the meat from the pot. Allow to cool slightly then remove from the bone. Purée the meat and lentil mixture (*see* Tip).

8 Combine half the fried onions with all the aubergines in a food processor and blend well.

9 Stir the two mixtures together in a pot, adding around 2–3 tablespoons of the *kashk* (or sour cream). Season with salt to taste and keep warm.

10 Heat 5–6 tablespoons oil in a small pan. Add the chopped garlic and sauté until golden. Rub the dried mint to a powder between your fingers and add to the pan. Stir just twice and remove the pan from the heat immediately (otherwise the mint will taste bitter).

11 Dissolve the ground saffron by stirring it into 3 tablespoons of hot water.

12 Spread the meat and aubergine mixture on a platter. Distribute the remaining *kashk* on top, and sprinkle over the chopped walnuts and the remaining onions.

13 To finish, drizzle the dish decoratively with the garlic-mint oil and the saffron water.

TIP: Traditionally, the meat is pounded with the other ingredients with a mortar and pestle until everything is well mixed. A potato masher, hand-held blender or processor may also be used, but take care not to purée the mixture too finely.

NOTE: *Halim* was once a typical winter breakfast dish. Its classic preparation was highly involved: first, a whole lamb was cooked in a huge pot. The bones were then removed, and the meat, fat and tail were transferred to another pot and cooked in their own juices, together with wheat groats. The cooking would take place overnight, and constant stirring was needed, so the family members all had to take turns. This is how the job of the *halim-pazi* came about: a person who would display the pre-cooked whole lamb on a large salver in the bazaar the day before it was to be eaten, often garnished with oranges and vegetables, and impressively illuminated, before preparing it overnight to serve for breakfast the next day.

VARIATION: *Kashk-o bademjan* is a meatless variation of this dish. Simply substitute additional aubergines for the lamb. The method of preparation remains the same, but pounding the lentils is a much easier job without the meat, making this vegetarian variant of *halim* the simplest to make.

MIRZAGHASEMI
AUBERGINE (EGGPLANT) AND EGG PURÉE

SERVES 4 AS A MAIN COURSE, 8 AS AN APPETIZER
5–6 small aubergines (eggplants), approx 600g/1lb 5oz
1 garlic bulb
oil
1/2 teaspoon turmeric
4 eggs
salt

1 Preheat the oven to 200°C/400°F/gas mark 6.
2 Wash and dry the aubergines, and prick each one in several places with a fork (this will prevent them from exploding in the oven).
3 Bake the aubergines in the oven, turning frequently. When the skin starts to blacken and come away from the flesh in places, take the aubergines out and leave them until cool enough to handle. Peel off the skin using your fingers or a sharp knife. If it comes away easily, the aubergines are cooked. Bits that do not peel away easily can be removed under warm running water.
4 Peel and finely chop the garlic cloves.
5 Heat some oil in a large pan over a medium flame.

Add half the garlic, and fry for 1 minute, so that it colours slightly. Sprinkle with the turmeric.
6 Add the grilled, skinned aubergines and fry uncovered, stirring occasionally, until all the liquid from the aubergines has evaporated, and you are left with a fairly firm mixture.
7 While the aubergines are frying, crack the eggs into a bowl, season with salt, and beat thoroughly.
8 With a wooden spoon, open up a space in the aubergine mixture about the size of your palm and pour in a drop of oil. As soon as the oil is hot, add the remaining garlic and fry until golden. Push the garlic slightly away from the centre and add the eggs.
9 After 2 minutes, mix everything with the aubergines and continue frying the mixture for a few minutes more.

TIP: Serve with warmed, crisp Persian flatbread (*lavash*) and fresh herbs.

NOTE: This dish comes from northern Iran, and is often prepared with masses of fresh garlic.

ABDUGH KHIAR
CHILLED YOGURT SOUP

SERVES 4 AS AN APPETIZER
400ml (14fl oz) yogurt
1 cucumber
12 walnut halves
50g (1 3/4oz) golden sultanas
salt, pepper
4 tablespoons fresh mint (or 2 tablespoons dried mint)
1 tablespoon dried rose petals (available in Persian shops)

1 Pour the yogurt into a large bowl. Peel and grate the cucumber, and add it to the yogurt.
2 Place the walnut halves in a small bowl and scald with boiling water; let stand for 10 minutes, drain, and remove the skin with a pointed knife. Finely chop the skinned walnuts with a large knife.

3 Stir the sultanas and chopped nuts into the yogurt, adding salt and pepper to taste. If you are using dried mint, rub it between your fingers to a powdery consistency and add it at this stage. If you are using fresh mint, wash it just before serving, shake it dry, remove the stalks, finely chop the leaves, and mix with the yogurt.
4 Leave the soup to sit for at least 1 hour to let the flavours combine. Serve sprinkled with the rose petals and the mint.

TIP: *Abdugh khiar* is a popular appetizer. On warm days, you could also serve this dish as a main course chilled soup for 2 people. Thin the yogurt with 175ml (6fl oz) of iced water, adding a few ice-cubes just before serving. Serve with lots of crisp, fresh Persian flatbread.

MAST-O KHIAR
YOGURT AND CUCUMBER

SERVES 4 AS AN APPETIZER OR SIDE DISH

1 cucumber
salt, pepper
400ml (14fl oz) yogurt
3–4 tablespoons dried mint
1 garlic clove (optional)

1 Peel and coarsely grate the cucumber.
2 Put the grated cucumber into a sieve, sprinkle with salt, and allow to drain for about 10 minutes. Squeeze it out well against the sides of the sieve and transfer to a bowl. Add the yogurt and stir, so that everything is mixed well together.
3 Rub the dried mint to a fine powder between your fingers and stir into the yogurt. Season generously with salt and pepper.
4 To decorate the yogurt, simply powder a little more dried mint and sprinkle on top in a random pattern before serving.

TIP: If you like, you could add 1 crushed garlic clove to the mixture. In Tehran, the garlic is usually omitted.

MAST-O MUSIR
YOGURT WITH WILD GARLIC

SERVES 4 AS AN APPETIZER OR SIDE DISH

3 tablespoons dried *musir* (wild garlic)
400ml (14fl oz) yogurt
salt, pepper

1 Place the dried *musir* slices in a large bowl. Cover with enough cold water to allow for the wild garlic slices to swell to about twice their size. Soak overnight in the refrigerator.
2 Very finely chop the soaked *musir*. The more finely the wild garlic is chopped, the better its flavour will combine with the yogurt.
3 Mix the yogurt and chopped *musir* thoroughly, add salt and pepper to taste, and serve.

TIP: *Musir* is known in the UK as wild garlic. Although it tastes similar to garlic, it is considerably milder and, significantly, is much easier to digest.

NOTE: *Mast-o musir* is easy to prepare, and makes a typical Persian appetizer when served with a little flatbread. It is also frequently served as an accompaniment to *chelo* and *kebab,* and is equally delicious served as a dip with salted crisps.

Following page: Window in an old townhouse belonging to the Tabatabei merchant family of Kashan.

BORANI ESFENAJ

SPINACH WITH YOGURT

SERVES 4 AS AN APPETIZER OR SIDE DISH

600g (1lb 5oz) fresh spinach or 300g (10^1/$_2$oz) frozen
  leaf spinach
1 large onion
oil
^{1}/$_2$ teaspoon turmeric
300ml (10fl oz) yogurt (preferably Greek yogurt with
  10 per cent fat)
^{1}/$_2$ teaspoon cinnamon

1 Wash the fresh spinach carefully in several changes
of water, then trim, removing the coarse stalks, and shake
the leaves dry. (If using frozen spinach, place in a sieve
and drain it well.) Stack the leaves and cut them into very
thin strips.

2 Place the spinach in a pot, cover, and stew it in its
own juices (without adding any water or fat) for around
6–7 minutes, until almost done. Then drain, gently
pressing the leaves against the sides of the sieve with a
spoon to squeeze out the excess moisture.

3 Finely chop the onion. Heat some oil in a large pan and
sauté until golden. Sprinkle the turmeric onto the onion
and stir once. Tip half the sautéed onions into a small bowl
and set aside.

4 Add the drained spinach to the remaining onions in
the pan, and fry, without covering, over a medium heat for
7–10 minutes, stirring occasionally. Transfer the spinach
and onion mixture to a bowl and leave to cool.

5 Once the spinach has cooled completely, add the yogurt,
stir well, and sprinkle with the reserved onions.

6 Just before serving, dust the top with cinnamon and
hand round fresh *lavash* (flatbread) to accompany the dip.

VARIATION: Peel and finely chop 2 garlic cloves. Briefly
sauté the garlic in a little oil at the same time as the onion,
but in a separate small pan, until the scent rises. Add the
garlic to the spinach and onion mixture, and continue as
described in the recipe. For an intensely garlicky flavour,
the garlic can also be pressed raw through a garlic press
into the cooled yogurt-spinach mixture.

BORANI BADEMJAN

AUBERGINE (EGGPLANT) YOGURT

SERVES 4 AS AN APPETIZER OR SIDE DISH

3–4 small aubergines (eggplants), approx 400g (14oz)
300ml (10fl oz) yogurt (preferably Greek yogurt with
  10 per cent fat)
5 garlic cloves

1 Preheat the oven to 200°C/400°F/gas mark 6.

2 Wash and dry the aubergines. Prick each one several
times with a fork.

3 Bake the aubergines in the oven, turning frequently to
expose all sides evenly to the heat. When the skin begins
to turn black and lift away from the flesh in places, remove
the aubergines from the oven and allow them to cool until
they can be handled. Peel off the skin using your fingers or
a sharp knife. If the aubergines are done, the skin will
easily come away from the flesh. Stubborn pieces of skin

can be removed by holding the aubergines briefly under
warm running water.

4 Once they are completely cooled, mash the flesh of
the aubergines thoroughly with a fork. Mix the mashed
flesh in a bowl with the yogurt until you obtain a
smooth mixture.

5 Peel the garlic cloves and crush them into the yogurt
and aubergine mixture, stirring well to combine. Allow
the aubergine-yogurt to stand for at least 1 hour so that
all the flavours mingle, then serve it with some warm,
crisp flatbread.

TIP: The fresher and stronger the garlic, the better this
dish will taste. Garlic that contains a green shoot is no
longer very fresh, but can still be used if the shoot is
removed first.

SALAD-E SHIRAZI

TOMATO AND CUCUMBER SALAD

SERVES 4 AS A SIDE DISH

1 cucumber

2 tomatoes

1 shallot

2 tablespoons freshly squeezed lemon juice

2 tablespoons olive oil

salt, freshly ground black pepper

1 Peel the cucumber and dice into small pieces (about 0.5 cm/¼-inch square). Wash the tomatoes and dice as evenly as possible into pieces of a similar size.

2 Chop the shallot very finely and transfer to a bowl with the diced cucumber and tomato. Add lemon juice, olive oil, salt and pepper.

3 Gently mix all the ingredients, allowing the salad to stand for about 30 minutes before serving, so that the flavours have time to mingle.

TIP: The ratio of cucumber to tomato used in this salad is a matter of taste. If you can get hold of flavourful tomatoes, then increase the proportion. Cocktail tomatoes (large cherry tomatoes still on the vine), which are frequently more aromatic, as well as firmer, can also be used to good effect.

NOTE: *Salad-e shirazi*, a salad that is as simple as it is delicious, is very popular throughout Iran — a truly classic dish.

SALAD-E OLIVIEH

CHICKEN SALAD

SERVES 2 AS A MAIN COURSE,

4 AS AN APPETIZER

2 chicken legs

1 onion, peeled

2 bay leaves

½ teaspoon turmeric

salt, white pepper

3 large, waxy (salad) potatoes

2 eggs

250g (9oz) pickled gherkins

60g (2¼oz) peas, cooked or canned

1 large carrot

3 tablespoons mayonnaise

2–3 tablespoons lemon juice (or vinegar)

2 tomatoes (optional)

1 Rinse the chicken legs in cold water, place in a pot, and pour over 500ml (18fl oz) water. Add the onion, bay leaves and turmeric, and season with salt. Cover the pot and poach the meat for about 1½ hours, until tender.

2 Meanwhile, cook the potatoes until just tender, then peel and grate them coarsely (or dice into small pieces).

Transfer to a large bowl. Hard-boil the eggs for 10 minutes, then run under cold water and remove the shells. Finely chop the eggs and add to the potatoes in the bowl. Cut the pickled gherkins into small dice, and add to the potatoes along with the peas.

3 Lift the cooked chicken legs from the stock, reserving the liquid. Pull the meat gently from the bones, discarding the skin. Cut the meat into small pieces and add to the potato, egg and vegetable mixture.

4 Peel the carrot and cook in the chicken stock for about 10 minutes (until *al dente*), then chop finely and add to the salad mixture.

5 Thoroughly mix the mayonnaise and lemon juice (or vinegar), add salt and pepper to taste, then pour the mixture over the salad ingredients and gently fold in. Add a little cold chicken stock if desired.

6 Arrange the salad in a shallow bowl and serve accompanied by fresh flatbread. A few slices of tomato make a suitable garnish.

VARIATION: For a lighter variation, use chicken breast instead of the chicken legs. The mayonnaise can be replaced by 1 tablespoon olive oil.

KUKU SABZI
HERB OMELETTE

SERVES 4 AS A MAIN COURSE, 8 AS AN APPETIZER

large bunches (sufficient to fill one good cup when chopped) fresh herbs (flat-leaf parsley, dill, coriander and chives, in roughly equal proportions)

1–2 tablespoons barberries (to taste)

8 eggs

1 tablespoon flour

6 walnut halves, coarsely chopped (to taste)

oil

salt

1 Wash the herbs and shake them dry. Remove the stalks from the parsley, dill and coriander, add the chives and chop as finely as possible.

2 Tip the dried barberries onto a plate and sort through them, removing any tiny stones. Rinse the berries in cold running water and drain well.

3 Crack the eggs into a bowl, beat them, and stir in the flour to produce a smooth mixture.

4 Add the chopped herbs to the eggs and season with salt. Carry on beating for a further 10 minutes. Stir in the walnuts and barberries.

5 Heat a little oil in a large, non-stick pan with a lid. Pour in the egg batter, cover with the lid and slowly brown over a low heat for 30 minutes. The beaten egg mixture will rise in the pan, so that the *kuku* looks almost like a cake.

6 To brown the *kuku* on the other side, remove the lid after 30 minutes and place a large plate upside-down over the pan. Turn the pan over with the plate on top, giving it a gentle shake if necessary. The *kuku* will now be crust-side up on the plate. Now slide it back gently into the pan, browned side up, cover again, and cook for a further 10 minutes over a low-to-medium heat, until done.

7 Serve with yogurt and flatbread.

TIP: When young spinach, cress, or fresh wild garlic are available, these are excellent combined with herbs to taste – the important thing is to use 3 or 4 different types of herbs in fairly equal amounts.

NOTE: *Kuku sabzi* with walnuts and barberries is very popular among the *Azeri* (an ethnic group in Iran). The barberries are pleasantly tart, and the quantity used can be varied according to taste.

Right: A typical family scene behind the high walls in the old town of Yazd.

KUKU-YE BADEMJAN
AUBERGINE (EGGPLANT) OMELETTE

SERVES 4–6 AS A MAIN COURSE,
8–10 AS AN APPETIZER

5–6 small aubergines (eggplants), approx 600g/1lb 5oz
1 onion
1 teaspoon turmeric
6 eggs
groundnut oil
salt

1 Preheat oven to 200°C/400°F/gas mark 6.
2 Wash and dry the aubergines (eggplants) and prick each one in several places with a fork, to prevent them from exploding in the oven.
3 Bake the aubergines in the oven, turning them frequently. When the skin starts to blacken and comes away from the flesh in places, take the aubergines out and leave them until they are cool enough to handle. Now peel off the skin using your fingers or a sharp knife. If it comes away easily, the aubergines are done. Any bits that do not peel away easily can be removed under warm running water. Pat the aubergines dry and chop into small pieces with a sharp, broad-bladed knife.
4 Finely chop the onions and fry in a small pan in a little oil until golden. Sprinkle with turmeric, stir once and set aside.
5 Crack the eggs into a bowl and beat until frothy.
6 Add the chopped aubergine and the cooled onions to the eggs, stir well and season with salt.
7 Heat a little oil in a large non-stick pan. Pour in the egg mixture, cover the pan, and let everything brown slowly over a low heat for 30 minutes: the beaten egg mixture will rise in the pan, so that the finished *kuku* looks almost like a cake.
8 To brown the *kuku* on the other side, remove the lid after 30 minutes and place a large plate upside-down over the pan. Turn the pan over with the plate on top, giving it a gentle shake if necessary. The *kuku* will now be crust-side-up on the plate. Slide it back into the pan, browned side up, cover again, and cook for a further 10 minutes over a low-to-medium heat, until done.
9 Serve with yogurt and flatbread.

TIP: Cut the aubergine omelet into wedges like a cake and serve with yogurt and fresh flatbread.

VARIATIONS: For *kuku-ye kadu*, substitute courgettes (zucchini) for the aubergines. Wash and peel the courgettes and cut them into 1-cm (1/2-inch) slices. Sprinkle the slices with salt and leave them to drain for about an hour in a large colander, or on a paper towel. Then pat them dry and fry them in batches in groundnut oil until golden brown. Finely chop the fried courgettes and add to the egg mixture. Continue as described in the recipe for *kuku-ye bademjan* (aubergine/eggplant omelet).

For *kuku-ye golkalam*, use cauliflower. Before cooking, soak the cauliflower briefly in salted water to clean it and get rid of any bugs. Next, cut out the stalk, divide the cauliflower into florets and cook in plenty of boiling, salted water for 10 minutes until crisp tender. Drain, and chop into small pieces. Add the cauliflower to the egg mixture (there is no need to fry it first), and continue as above.

Right: Herbs are offered for sale in huge bundles.

Opposite: To help the household to identify callers, there are separate door-knockers for men and women.

DOLMEH FELFEL

STUFFED PEPPERS

SERVES 4 AS A MAIN COURSE, 8 AS AN APPETIZER

4 large red, green or yellow peppers

2 large, firm tomatoes

FOR THE STUFFING:

50g (1³/₄oz) *lapeh* (yellow lentils)

100g (3¹/₂oz) rice

2 small onions

oil

1 teaspoon turmeric

250g (9oz) minced (ground) beef

large bunches (sufficient to fill one good cup when chopped)
  fresh herbs (dill, tarragon, flat-leaf parsley, chives, mint
  in roughly equal proportions). If using dried herbs, allow
  about one-quarter the weight of fresh herbs.

1 tablespoon tomato paste

salt, pepper

juice of 2 lemons

1–2 tablespoons sugar

¹/₂ teaspoon saffron, ground

FOR THE TOMATO SAUCE:

1kg (2lb 4oz or about 8 medium-sized) beefsteak tomatoes

50g (1³/₄oz) parsley (1 small bunch)

1 tablespoon butter

1 scant tablespoon flour

salt, pepper

1 garlic clove

1 teaspoon sugar

¹/₂ teaspoon vinegar

1 Pour boiling water over the *lapeh* (yellow lentils) and soak overnight. The next day, strain and rinse with one change of fresh water. Place in a pot and cover generously with fresh water. Cook at a rolling boil for 15–20 minutes, then strain through a sieve.

2 For the tomato sauce, coarsely shred the tomatoes using a grater. Wash the parsley and shake dry; discard the stalks and finely chop the leaves.

3 Heat the butter in a non-stick pan. Add the flour and sweat for 3–4 minutes over a medium heat, until golden. Pour in the grated tomatoes and season with salt and pepper. Add the garlic clove, chopped parsley, sugar, and vinegar and simmer, covered, for about 30 minutes over a low-to-medium heat.

4 For the stuffing, first wash the rice. Bring 1 litre (35fl oz) water to the boil, tip in the rice, and simmer gently for 5–6 minutes until *al dente*. Drain well.

5 Meanwhile, slice the tops off the peppers and tomatoes just below the stalks. Reserve the tops to use as 'lids'. Carefully scrape out the cores, seeds and membranes with a spoon, taking care not to damage the outer wall of the vegetables.

6 Returning to the sauce, finely chop the onions. Heat a little oil in a large pan and sauté the onions over a medium heat until golden. Sprinkle with turmeric and stir, then add the meat and continue frying everything over a medium heat for around 15 minutes, stirring occasionally.

7 Meanwhile, wash and shake dry the fresh herbs, discard the stalks, and finely chop the leaves. If using dried herbs, rub these to a fine powder between your fingers.

8 Add the lentils, rice, tomato paste, and chopped herbs to the meat, stir everything to combine, and continue frying for a further 5 minutes over a low heat.

9 Next, add 250ml (9fl oz) water, and gently braise with the lid on for a further 20 minutes, or until all the liquid is absorbed.

10 Season the meat mixture with salt, pepper, lemon juice, sugar, and saffron, and gently braise for another 10 minutes. The stuffing should have a sweet-and-sour flavour as well as an element of heat.

11 Stuff the peppers and tomatoes with the meat mixture. Arrange them side by side in a large pot or saucepan, standing upright but not too close together, and replace the 'lids'. Pour in the tomato sauce and 250ml (9fl oz) hot water. Bring the pan briefly to the boil, cover and gently simmer over a low heat for 45 minutes.

VARIATION: You can also stuff aubergines (eggplants) in this manner (*dolmeh bademjan*): Prepare the stuffing and tomato sauce as described above, reserving 2–3 tomatoes. Top the stuffed aubergines with the tomatoes, sliced into thin rounds. Bake in a preheated oven for about 40 minutes at 180°C/350°F/gas mark 4.

DOLMEH BARG-E MOU
STUFFED VINE LEAVES

MAKES ABOUT 40

60g (2¼oz) *lapeh* (yellow lentils)

1 x jar (about 350g/12oz net weight) vine leaves in brine

180g (5¾oz) rice

1 large onion

oil

1 teaspoon turmeric

400g (14oz) minced (ground) beef

large bunches (sufficient to fill one good cup when chopped) fresh herbs (basil, dill, tarragon, wild garlic, mint, flat-leaf parsley and chives — *see* Tip)

salt, pepper

juice of 2 lemons

2 tablespoons sugar

1 teaspoon saffron, ground

1 teaspoon butter

1 Wash the *lapeh*, pour over enough boiling water to cover generously and leave to soak overnight. The next day, drain the lentils in a sieve and rinse in one change of fresh water. Tip the lentils into a pan, add water to cover, and parboil for 30 minutes.

2 Drain and separate the vine leaves and stack them flat on a plate, ready for use.

3 Wash the rice. Bring 1 litre (35fl oz) of water to the boil and cook the rice for 4–6 minutes, until *al dente*, then strain.

4 Finely chop the onion. Heat a little oil in a large pan and fry over a medium heat until golden. Sprinkle with the turmeric, add the minced (ground) beef, and fry everything for 15 minutes, stirring occasionally.

5 Meanwhile, wash and shake the herbs dry, cut off the stalks, and finely chop just the leaves. If using dried mint, rub to a powder between your fingers.

6 Add the lentils, rice and herbs to the meat and continue frying everything for another 5 minutes, then pour in 250ml (9fl oz) water and bring to the boil. Reduce to a low heat and gently braise the meat, covered, for around 30 minutes, until all the liquid is absorbed.

7 Season generously with salt and pepper, half the lemon juice, 1 tablespoon sugar, and ½ teaspoon saffron. The stuffing should have a sweet-and-sour flavour and the merest hint of heat.

8 Pour 1–2 tablespoons oil into a large non-stick pan, tilting the pan to distribute the oil evenly. Now cover the bottom of the pan with flat vine leaves. This will stop the stuffed vine leaves from sticking to the pan.

9 Cut away the stalk of each vine leaf with a sharp knife. To wrap the stuffing in the vine leaves, you'll need one large leaf per *dolmeh* – if the leaves are small, overlap 2 leaves, so that you have a rollable shape. Place about 2 teaspoons of the stuffing in the centre, then roll up the leaf halfway, turn in both sides, and finish rolling tautly. Place the *dolmeh* seam-side down and fill the pan halfway up with two or three layers of *dolmeh*.

10 Mix together 250ml (9fl oz) of hot water, 1 teaspoon salt, ½ teaspoon saffron, and the remaining sugar and lemon juice, and pour over the *dolmeh*. Dot with butter.

11 Place a plate that is slightly smaller than the circumference of the pan upside-down on top of the *dolmeh* and replace the lid.

12 Bring the water to the boil over a medium heat; reduce at once to low, and simmer very gently for 1 hour. Remove the pan from the heat, take off the lid, and carefully remove the plate.

13 Let the *dolmeh* cool slightly, then remove from the pan, taking care not to damage the leaves. Serve arranged on a large plate.

TIP: If fresh mint is not available, substitute 1 tablespoon dried mint. If you are using dried herbs, always reckon on allowing about one-quarter the weight of the fresh herbs.

NOTE: Although it originated in Turkey, *dolmeh* has been a popular dish in Persia for centuries. Any vegetable that is suitable for stuffing, either by being hollowed out or being used as a wrapping, can be transformed into a *dolmeh* dish with the filling described above, for example, peppers, tomatoes, aubergines (eggplants), apples, quinces, or cucumbers. White cabbage leaves make an interesting substitute for vine leaves.

Following pages: On Fridays, places like this are popular destinations for family outings – perfect for a lavish picnic.

TORSHI FELFEL SABZ

PICKLED HOT PEPPERS

MAKES 1–2 JARS

500g (1lb 2oz) hot peppers (small green variety)
about 500ml (18fl oz) white wine vinegar

1 Wash and dry the hot peppers. Distribute them evenly into some clean, sterilized jars with a tight seal.

2 Fill the jars with a good, strong wine vinegar and seal them tightly.

3 Store the jars in a cool, dark place for at least 3 months before sampling. The pickled hot peppers will keep for at least a year. If anything, their flavour will only improve with age.

TORSHI SIR

PICKLED GARLIC

MAKES 2–3 LARGE JARS

1kg (2¼lb) whole, young garlic bulbs
about 750ml (26fl oz) red wine vinegar

1 Fill clean, sterilized jars with fresh, young garlic bulbs – whole, or halved if necessary, but leave the skin on.
2 Fill the jars with a good, strong red wine vinegar and seal tightly.

3 Store the jars in a cool, dark place for at least a year.

TIP: This *torshi* is ready after a year, but remains good for 2, 3, or even 5 years – in fact, the longer it's left, the darker it turns, and the better it tastes. Although the peel of the garlic bulb cannot be eaten, even in the case of aged *torshi sir*, it can be removed very easily, and leaving it on while the garlic is pickling improves the taste.

TORSHI ANBEH

PICKLED MANGO

MAKES 2–3 LARGE JARS

6 mangoes
salt
8 hot red chilli peppers
5 garlic cloves
2 tablespoons oil
1 tablespoon fresh ginger, peeled and chopped
1 teaspoon ground coriander
1 tablespoon coarsely ground black pepper (alternatively, grind in a mortar, or use whole peppercorns)
1 teaspoon mustard powder (or ground brown mustard seeds)
1 teaspoon black cumin seed
1 teaspoon turmeric
strong white wine vinegar (for filling jars)

1 Peel the mangoes and cut the flesh into bite-size pieces. Sprinkle some salt on a plate and turn the pieces of mango in it.
2 Wash the hot chilli peppers and slit open lengthways. Remove the seeds and membranes, and cut the flesh diagonally into very thin strips. Peel and halve the cloves of garlic.
3 Heat the oil in a pan. Add the chillies and garlic and fry briefly over a medium heat until they become fragrant. Immediately remove from the heat, then add the remaining spices to the pan and stir. Remove the mangoes from the salt, shake off well, and stir into the spices in the pan.
4 Pour into clean, sterilized jars and fill with strong white wine vinegar before sealing tightly (*see* Tip).

TIP: The mango *torshi* is ready after just one month, but can equally be kept for much longer. *Torshi* should only be made when a particular vegetable or fruit is in season – for pickled garlic in particular, you need small, young, juicy garlic bulbs. The vinegar used for *torshi* must be concentrated, otherwise the contents will go off quickly. For this reason, balsamic or mild wine vinegars are not suitable.

NOTE: *Torshi* is the name given to vegetables or fruit pickled in vinegar and salt. It is served alongside various Persian dishes as a side dish or *meze* (literally, 'a taste'). With good vegetables, and above all with a good vinegar, you can learn to enjoy and appreciate the acidity of this

dish, to which the European palate is not really accustomed. In addition, *torshi* has many fruity nuances. As well as the pleasant taste of a well-prepared *torshi*, it has a beneficial effect on the digestion: the acidity helps the stomach to digest fat – a good reason why Persian cookery is hard to imagine without *torshi*.

Above: Those who visit the little mosque in Khor, at the edge of the great Kavir Desert, will be treated to a glass of tea by its kindly curator.

TAHINE

SESAME-PASTE DIP

SERVES 4–6 AS AN HORS D'OEUVRE

250ml (9fl oz) yogurt (Greek yogurt with 10 per cent fat)

4 tablespoons tahini paste (sesame paste, found in large supermarkets or in Greek food shops)

2–3 tablespoons freshly squeezed lemon juice

1 generous pinch ground cumin

salt, white pepper

6 large carrots

6 sticks celery

1 Place the yogurt in a bowl. Give the tahini paste a good stir in its jar to distribute the sesame oil evenly.

2 Combine 4 tablespoons tahini paste with the yogurt and season generously to taste with the lemon juice, ground cumin, salt and white pepper.

3 Decant the sesame-paste dip into small bowls before serving.

4 Wash and trim the carrots and celery, cut into long, thin sticks and serve with the dip.

ADASI

LENTIL DIP

SERVES 4–6 AS AN HORS D'OEUVRE

200g (7oz) *adas* (black caviar lentils)

oil

1 large onion

1 teaspoon turmeric

salt, pepper

1 The evening before you make the dish, sort through the lentils and wash them thoroughly; place in a large bowl and cover them with plenty of cold water. Leave to soak overnight. The next day, strain and rinse with one change of fresh water.

2 Finely chop the onion. Heat a little oil in a large pot and sauté the onion until golden. Sprinkle over the turmeric and stir once. Add the soaked, drained lentils along with 1 litre (35fl oz) of water.

3 Cover the lentils and cook for about 2–3 hours, topping up with water as and when necessary, and stirring now and again.

4 Finally, season the lentil purée generously with salt and pepper to taste.

TIP: Serve the lentil dip either warm or cold, accompanied by flatbread.

ZEYTUN PARVARDEH

MARINATED OLIVES

MAKES 1 LARGE JAR

250g (9oz) green olives

3 garlic cloves, peeled and coarsely chopped

1 tablespoon each dried oregano and dried mint, rubbed between your fingertips to a fine powder

1 teaspoon aniseed liqueur (or aniseed)

2–3 tablespoons vinegar

1 Place all ingredients in a bowl and mix well.

2 Pour into a clean, sterilized jar, seal tightly, and leave the olives in the refrigerator to marinate for a week.

Right: The oasis village of Chuachupan reflects the colour and light of the desert.

THICK SOUPS

ASH

Ash is one of the oldest Persian dishes. The consistency of this tradition-laden dish is somewhere between a soup and a stew – hence the description of 'thick soup'.

The word for 'cook' – *ashpaz* in the Persian language – illustrates the importance attached to this dish in Persian cookery. *Ash* is traditionally a poor man's dish.

Recipes for *ash* have been handed down since late Zoroastrian times. After the Arabs – and with them, Islam – had conquered Persia, the faith of the followers of Zoroaster lost its status as the official state religion. This brought about a worsening of the social position of Zoroastrians, and the poverty of the inhabitants of the cities of Yazd and Kerman, the two strongholds of the Zoroastrian faith, became proverbial.

Among the typical feast-day dishes of these poorer classes was a wheat soup (in the dialect of the day *ash-e gannom*), which was cooked overnight and served for breakfast. In the evening, pounded wheat was stirred into boiling water with a little meat, onions and seasonings. The cooking pot was lowered into a hole in the ground lined with glowing coals, covered with coarse straw, and left overnight. The following morning, the soup would be thick and ready to eat – all that was needed was to remove the meat from the bones, pound it with a large mortar, and stir it back into the soup.

The age-old native tradition of the thick soup has meant that more than 100 different varieties of *ash* have evolved, using a wide range of ingredients depending on the season and the region. The main components of *ash* are pulses and grains, with masses of fresh herbs. The quantity of herbs given in the recipes is geared to how fresh herbs are sold nowadays in Iran, as well as in our Asian or Greek food shops – i.e. in large bunches with their coarse stalks still attached. Once the herbs are de-stalked, washed, and finely chopped, you'll be left with a good half of the quantity given in the recipe to add to the pot.

Ash must be allowed to cook for a long time, ideally four to five hours. Unfortunately, these days we rarely have the option of burying a pot with glowing coals, a technique that reduces the risk of the food catching and burning. For this reason, the dish needs to be stirred frequently, adding more water as necessary.

Personally, I am always delighted when my mother surprises me with a batch of *ash*, so that I do not have to find time to cook it myself. There is *ash* with fruit, such as *ash-e alu* (with prunes) or *ash-e anar* (with pomegranate) or with vegetables, such as *ash-e bademjan* (with aubergine/eggplant). It can also be made with pulses, for example *ash-e sholehqalamkar* (with chickpeas and white beans) or with grain, such as *ash-ejo* (with barley), or the popular *ash-e reshteh* with special thick noodles only available in Iran or in Persian shops.

The latter is a traditional dish, usually prepared as one part of the menu on special occasions, such as a substantial dinner during a period of fasting. One of the most popular occasions for serving *ash-e reshteh* is at a farewell celebration for a family member: if the person is going away for a long time, an *ash-e reshteh-ye posht-e pa* will be cooked. This means, literally, 'a thick noodle soup behind the foot' – that is, after his departure. Generally, this is cooked on the third or fifth day after the departure of the loved one, in the hope that he will not be gone for too long. The soup is also distributed to the neighbours as a reminder of the absent person, and to wish him good health.

Left: Built by Karim Khan in Shiraz, the *Hammam-e Vakil* was recently converted into a traditional tea-house and restaurant.

ASH-E RESHTEH
NOODLE SOUP

SERVES 4–6

100g (3½oz) each dried peas and dried red kidney beans
100g (3½oz) *adas* (lentils)
2 large onions
oil
2 teaspoons turmeric
3 tablespoons dried mint
large bunches (sufficient to fill 2 good cups when
    chopped) fresh herbs (coriander, flat-leaf parsley, chives
    and spinach in about equal proportions)
4 tablespoons *kashk* (or sour cream)
200g (7oz) *ash* noodles (available in Persian shops)
1 tablespoon flour
3 garlic cloves

1 Soak the pulses overnight in plenty of cold water to
cover. The following day, strain, then rinse in one change
of fresh water.

2 Finely chop the onions. Heat a little oil in a large
non-stick pan and fry over a medium heat until golden.
Sprinkle over the turmeric and stir once, then take the pan
off the heat. Remove half the onions and set aside in a
small bowl to use later in the garnish.

3 Have 1 litre (35fl oz) hot water at the ready. Crumble
the dried mint to a fine powder between your fingers.
Place the pan with the onions back on the heat and add
1 tablespoon of the mint. Fry briefly, stirring continuously,
until the scent of the mint rises. Immediately pour in the
hot water.

4 Add the pulses to the pan and bring to the boil. Boil for
10 minutes. Reduce the heat, cover, and simmer for 1½
hours, adding more water as necessary.

5 Meanwhile, wash and shake dry the herbs. Remove the
stalks from the parsley, coriander, and spinach, and finely
chop all the leaves, together with the chives.

6 Boil the *kashk*, if using, with 250ml (9fl oz) water in
a small pan over a medium heat, stirring frequently to
prevent sticking. Cover and set aside.

7 Once the pulses are soft (about 1½ hours), pour in
1 more litre (35fl oz) hot water, season with salt, and bring
briefly to the boil. Add the chopped herbs to the pulses in
the pan, stir well, and bring to the boil once more.

8 Reduce the heat, cover the pot, and simmer gently for
30 minutes.

9 Next, slowly add the noodles into the pan, stirring
carefully.

10 Dissolve the flour in 125ml (4fl oz) cold water and
gently stir into the soup.

11 Cover the pot and simmer the contents gently for a
further 30 minutes, until the soup has reached a thick
consistency, adding a little hot water occasionally, if
necessary.

12 For the garnish, peel and finely chop the garlic cloves.
Heat a little oil in a small pan over a medium heat, add
the garlic, and sauté until golden, then immediately
transfer to a small bowl.

13 In another small pan, heat 2–3 tablespoons oil until
very hot, but do not allow it to smoke. Sprinkle in the
remaining dried mint, stir twice, until the mint aroma
rises, then remove the pan from the heat at once and
transfer the sautéed mint to a small bowl.

14 To decorate, heat the prepared *kashk* (or the sour
cream) to melting point and spoon it onto the *ash* in a
sweeping shape. Sprinkle the sautéed garlic, mint oil and
onions on top, using a small spoon.

TIP: Serve the *ash* in a large, attractive soup tureen.

NOTE: *Kashk* is a very special ingredient, and imparts
a specific taste to dishes; for this reason, there is no exact
substitute for it. You'll find jars of *kashk* (*see* illustration
on page 62) in any Persian shop, but nowhere else. Sour
cream is readily available and is therefore suggested as a
substitute for *kashk* in these recipes. Some types of fresh
cheese (all with a high fat content and containing no
gelatine) can be warmed to melting point and, similarly,
make a passable substitute. In both taste and consistency,
these soft cheeses and sour cream are reminiscent of *kashk*.
Unopened, *kashk* will keep for a long time in a jar, and
once opened it can be stored in a refrigerator for several
weeks. *Kashk* should never be consumed raw; before use,
it needs to be diluted with water – 4–5 tablespoons *kashk*
to 180–250ml (6¼–9fl oz) of water – and boiled for
20 minutes, stirring frequently and taking care that it
does not burn.

ASH-E SHOLEHQALAMKAR
BEGGAR'S SOUP

SERVES 8

150g (5^1/₂oz) each dried chickpeas, *adas* (lentils)
   and small white beans
salt, pepper
200g (7oz) rice
large bunches (sufficient to fill half a cup when chopped)
   fresh herbs (coriander, flat-leaf parsley, chives in about
   equal proportions)
50g (3^3/₄oz) spinach
6 onions
1kg (2^1/₄lb) lamb shoulder or leg (with bone)
1 teaspoon turmeric
2 tablespoons dried mint
3 tablespoons *kashk* (or sour cream)
oil

1 Wash all the pulses and soak overnight in cold water.
The following day, drain and rinse in one change of
fresh water.
2 Place the pulses in a large pot with 1 litre (35fl oz)
water, bring to the boil for 10 minutes, then simmer for a
further 50 minutes. Season with salt, then simmer for a
further 20 minutes.
3 Meanwhile, wash the rice and soak in cold water for
about 1 hour.
4 Wash the herbs and spinach and shake dry. Remove all
the stalks and finely chop the leaves together with the chives.
5 Cut the lamb into medium-sized cubes. Rub the dried
mint to a fine powder between your fingers.
6 Peel and finely chop the onions. Heat a little oil in a
large pan, add the onions, and fry over a medium heat until
golden. Sprinkle with the turmeric and 1 tablespoon of the
mint, and continue cooking briefly, stirring. As soon as the
scent of the mint rises, remove the pan from the heat. Take
out 1 heaped tablespoon of the onion mixture and set aside
in a small bowl for use later for the garnish.
7 Drain the pulses, then transfer them to a large pan
together with the lamb and the remaining onion mixture.
Pour over 1 litre (35fl oz) boiling water. Bring everything
to the boil, cover, and cook for 2 hours.
8 Lift out the lamb, remove the meat from the bone,
and using a pestle, pound it in a mortar or sturdy bowl.
Tip the pounded meat back into the soup. Add the drained
rice and chopped herbs, season with salt and pepper, and
cook gently for another hour, stirring from time to time to
prevent the thick soup from sticking.

9 While the soup is simmering, put the *kashk,* if using,
into a small saucepan and mix with 250ml (9fl oz) water;
cook uncovered over a medium heat for about 30 minutes,
stirring occasionally. Cover and set aside.
10 Just before serving, prepare the garnish by heating
2 tablespoons oil in a small pan. Sprinkle the remaining
mint into the hot oil, stir just once and remove from the
heat (the mint must not be allowed to turn black or it
will have a bitter taste).
11 To serve, transfer the *ash* into a soup tureen and
top with the *kashk* (or sour cream), the mint, and the
remaining onions.

NOTE: *Ash-e sholehqalamkar* is prepared on religious
holidays, for example on the 21st day of *Ramadan*, on the
day commemorating the martyrdom of Imam Ali, and on
the tenth day of the mourning month of Moharram,
among others. It is made in generous quantities for this
reason, often because a guest has been invited, or some of
the *ash* will be distributed among the needy. As with other
types of *ash*, this dish reheats well. In Iran, people say *Ja
oftadeh* – 'the food has fallen in the (right) place' – when
the meal has been cooked long enough for the flavours of
all the ingredients to have blended together perfectly.

Below: Kashk, as sold in the jar in Persian shops.

ASH-E JO
THICK BARLEY SOUP

SERVES 8

250g (9oz) dried chickpeas

500g (1lb 4oz) lamb (with bone)

1 onion, peeled

1 teaspoon turmeric

2 teaspoons pepper

large bunches (sufficient to fill 2 good cups when
chopped) fresh herbs (dill, coriander, flat-leaf parsley, and
chives in about equal proportions)

salt

500g (1lb 2oz) whole, husked barley grains (pearl barley), or
even better, pot barley (available in wholefood stores)

oil

4 tablespoons *kashk* (or sour cream)

1 tablespoon dried mint

salt

1 Wash the chickpeas and soak overnight in a generous
amount of cold water. Rinse in one change of fresh water
before using.

2 Wash the lamb and pat dry. Place it in a large pot
with the onion, turmeric and pepper. Add 2 litres (7fl oz)
water and bring to the boil. Simmer, covered, for 1 hour.

3 Wash and shake dry the herbs. Remove and discard all
the stalks, then finely chop the herbs and set them aside.

4 Add the barley, drained chickpeas and herbs to the
meat, pour in 500ml (18fl oz) water, bring back to the
boil, and simmer everything gently for 2 hours.

5 Lift out the lamb, remove the meat from the bone, then
pound with a pestle in a large mortar or in a sturdy bowl.

6 Return the pounded meat to the pot, season to taste
with salt, and gently simmer over a low heat for a further
30 minutes.

7 Meanwhile, tip the jar of *kashk* into a small saucepan
with 250ml (9fl oz) water and cook, uncovered, over
low-to-medium heat for about 30 minutes, stirring
frequently to prevent the *kashk* from sticking.

8 Stir the *kashk* (or sour cream) into the barley soup,
cover, and keep warm over the lowest heat (do not allow
it to come back to the boil).

9 Just before serving, crush the dried mint to a fine
powder between your fingers. Heat 2 tablespoons oil in a
small pan, sprinkle in the mint, and stir briefly until the
scent rises. Immediately remove the pan from the heat so
that the mint does not turn black.

10 To serve, transfer the *ash-e jo* to a soup tureen and
serve with the sautéed mint sprinkled on top.

TIP: While the barley soup is cooking, keep on adding
water as necessary until you achieve the consistency of a
thick soup.

Right: The inhabitants of Kandovan dug their living
quarters directly into the soft tufastone. The caves serve
as grain stores and also provide shelter for their beasts.

TWO STORIES ABOUT KING KHOSRO NUSHIRVAN

From *A Thousand and One Nights*

One day, while hunting, the King of the Persians Khosro Nushirvan was suddenly separated from his retinue. It being a hot day, he became thirsty, and approached a cottage that he espied just ahead. A girl was standing in the door, and he asked her for a drink. The girl hastened into the house, mixed the juice of a sugar cane with water, and handed it to the King. As he drank, the Persian King noticed a little chaff in the water, which forced him to drink slowly. He therefore asked the girl why the water was so cloudy. The girl explained that she had deliberately mixed the chaff into the water to prevent the King gulping down the cold water too quickly and thereby doing himself a mischief. This answer pleased Nushirvan, for it showed that the girl was clever as well as sensible. King Nushirvan then enquired how many sugar canes she had juiced for the water. When he learned that a single cane had sufficed for the drink, he thought to himself that the village must be fairly prosperous if one cane provided so much sugar. After he returned home, therefore, he had the community's taxes raised.

The next time he returned to the village, he asked for water at the same cottage, and the same girl brought him some. This time, though, the girl was gone for a long time before she handed him the glass. When he enquired as to the reason for the delay, she answered: 'Today I used three sugar canes to sweeten your water, and it still was not quite sweet enough!' 'Why is that?' asked Nushirvan, and the girl answered: 'The King is no longer well-disposed towards us, so our prosperity and happiness have also decreased.' Hearing this, Nushirvan laughed heartily, lowered the taxes, and was so taken with the girl that he made her his wife.

A Thousand and One Nights. The 750th night,
retold according to the original.

From the book *Siyasat-Nameh* ('The Art of Government') by Abu'Ali Hassan Tusi Nezam ol-Molk

The story is told that one day, King Nushirvan the Just mounted his horse and went hunting with his retinue, and rode past a village. He saw an old man of 90 years planting a walnut in the ground. This astonished Nushirvan, since a walnut tree only bears fruit after 20 years. 'Tell me, old man,' he called, 'is that a walnut tree you're planting there?' 'Yes,' answered the man. The Ruler then spoke: 'How long are you actually intending to live, so that you can eat the fruit of this tree?' The old man said: 'They plant, we eat; we plant, they eat.' This answer pleased Nushirvan. 'Bravo!' He said, and immediately commanded his bursar to give the old man 1,000 dirham. The old man exclaimed: 'Mark, my Lord! No one harvests from this nut tree faster than I!' 'How so?' said the King. The old man responded: 'If I had not planted the tree and my Lord had not passed by, what happened to me would not have happened, and I would not have given this answer. Where else could my humble self have been able to find the 1,000 dirham?' 'Bravo! Bravo!' said Nushirvan, and his bursar immediately gave the man a further 2,000 dirham, since the word 'bravo' had been uttered twice by his lord and master.

Adapted from Siasset-Nameh in
'Traité de gouvernement composé pour le sultan Melik Chah...'
Hg. Ch. Schefer (publ). Paris, 1891.

King Khosro Nushirvan (AD 531–579) was reputed to have 12,000 women in his harem. He was a very popular ruler, and centuries later many stories of his greatness and affability were still being told – stories such as the one above. Abu' Ali Hassan Tusi Nezam ol-Molk (1019–1092) was Grand Vizier under the Seljuk Sultan Alp Arslan, and his son Malek-Shah.

ASH-E ALU

THICK SOUP WITH PRUNES

SERVES 4

100g (3¹/₂oz) *lapeh* (yellow lentils)

200g (7oz) rice

large bunches (sufficient to make 175g/6oz when chopped)
fresh herbs (coriander, flat-leaf parsley, chives in about
    equal proportions)

2 large onions

oil

1 teaspoon turmeric

¹/₄ teaspoon cinnamon (optional)

2 tablespoons dried mint

12 *alu* (prunes, available from Persian shops)

salt, pepper

4 garlic cloves

1 Soak the lentils overnight in a generous amount of cold water. The next day, drain then rinse in one change of fresh water.

2 Wash the rice and soak in cold water for 1 hour.

3 Wash and shake dry the fresh herbs. Remove the stalks and then finely chop all the herbs. Set aside in a cool place.

4 Finely chop one of the onions. Heat some oil in a large pan and fry the chopped onion until golden. Add the turmeric and cinnamon, if using, and stir again once, then sprinkle over the dried mint and stir once more. As soon as the scent of the mint rises, remove the pan from the heat.

5 Add the soaked lentils to the onion and mint mixture and pour in 2 litres (70fl oz) water. Return the pan to the heat, bring to the boil, cover, and simmer for 30 minutes.

6 Drain the rice and add to the soup pan with the herbs, prunes and salt and pepper to taste. Cover, and continue simmering everything gently for at least another hour.

7 Before serving, prepare the garnish: peel and finely chop the garlic cloves, removing any green shoots. Heat a little oil in a small pan and sauté the garlic until golden, then transfer to a small bowl.

8 Cut the remaining onion into thin rings. Heat a little oil in a small pan and fry the onion rings until golden.

9 To serve, transfer the *ash* to a large soup tureen and garnish with the garlic and onion rings.

Right: In early summer, pansies create a blaze of colour in Shiraz's Bagh-e Nazar park.

TIP: Add water as necessary until you obtain the consistency of a thick soup.

NOTE: Like many other varieties of *ash*, *ash-e alu* also has a medicinal use – it is traditionally administered to calm the nerves.

VARIATIONS: *Ash-e sadeh* (simple thick soup) and *ash-e anar* (thick soup with pomegranate syrup).

For *ash-e sadeh*, instead of the prunes, the juice of a large lemon is used as an acidifier; for *ash-e anar*, about 2–3 tablespoons of pomegranate syrup is used. The amount of acidifier used can be increased or decreased according to taste.

RICE DISHES

BERENJ: CHELO, KATEH AND POLO

Rice is the focal point of Persian cuisine. In Iran itself, a great many varieties of rice are grown, mainly in the northern region along the coast of the Caspian Sea. Here the humidity can reach ninety nine per cent during the warm seasons, which is ideal for the cultivation of rice. Even in seemingly dry areas such as the southwest around Shiraz, however, rice is planted if the ground holds sufficient water.

Rice originally comes from East and Southeast Asia. It was certainly brought to Persia in ancient times, and became a staple and the national dish under the Safavids. All varieties of rice grown in Iran are variants of basmati rice. Basmati rice is not cheap, and there are three quality criteria to keep in mind at the time of purchase: it must be as white as possible, have a strong fragrance, and be long-grained.

The rice varieties on offer differ greatly. Between the short, thick *champa* variety (which in the past was often used for *kateh* dishes) and the long, thin, exquisite *sadri* variety, there are many intermediate levels varying in shape, scent and colour. Iranians have various methods for increasing the keeping qualities of the rice and protecting it from moisture. In the north, for example, it is smoked, which gives it a quite distinctive taste. Often, too, the rice is mixed with a high proportion of salt and stored in large containers in a dry place. The containers are covered with a fabric that simultaneously absorbs the moisture of the rice and keeps away vermin.

Rice has different names in Persian cookery, depending on how it is prepared. The two simple variants of rice (which is called *berenj* in its raw state) are *kateh* and *chelo*. For *kateh*, the rice is put on to boil with a fixed ratio of water, and it absorbs this liquid completely. The preparation of *chelo* is a little more refined; the rice is first cooked until *al dente* in plenty of water, then drained in a sieve. As a second stage, it is then steamed with a little butter. Finally there is *polo,* which is prepared like *chelo*, but other ingredients such as meat, vegetables or pulses are added at the second stage. Whichever method of preparation is followed, Persian rice is always fluffy and quite dry; the individual grains of rice should fall loosely from the spoon.

In Iran, rice is always washed before it is prepared; this rids it of loose starch and prevents the grains from sticking together. The washed rice should be soaked for at least twenty five minutes before cooking, but can be left for several hours in plenty of water to which a little salt has been added. Soaking gives the finished rice a particularly long grain. A non-stick pan is recommended for all rice dishes.

Persian rice is cooked in two stages, and always for much longer than its minimal cooking time would require. In the first stage, the rice is cooked uncovered over a medium-to-high heat in plenty of water at a rolling boil until *al dente*. The rice should not cook through completely, but should retain a slightly granular bite when it is drained. This can be checked using the '*al dente*' test: from time to time, a few grains of rice should be taken out of the boiling water with a spoon and crushed between the fingers. A tiny firm kernel should remain. As soon as the rice has reached this stage, it is drained through a sieve.

This first cooking stage should last from three and ten minutes, depending on the variety of rice, how long the rice was soaked, and whether fairly moist, fairly dry or no ingredients at all are to be added to the rice at the second cooking stage. If moist ingredients are to be added, the rice is cooked for a shorter time in the first stage; with dry or no additional ingredients, the cooking time is a little longer.

In the second stage of cooking, the rice is layered in the pan, the bottom of which has been coated with a mixture of butter or oil, water, and seasoning. The lid is wrapped in a clean cloth to absorb the moisture and allow the added flavourings to penetrate most effectively in the hot steam, while the coveted golden-brown rice crust, the *tahdig* ('pot bottom') forms on the bottom of the pan.
It is important for the heat to be high at the outset, so that plenty of steam forms and the *tahdig* eventually becomes nice and crunchy. For the long cooking time, the temperature is drastically reduced – depending on the cooker, usually to a low, and sometimes even to the lowest possible setting. If the heat is too low, the *tahdig* will become soft rather than crunchy; if too high, the *tahdig* will burn. With a bit of practice, however, your crust will come out perfect!

CHELO
SIEVE RICE METHOD

SERVES 4
600g (1lb 5oz) basmati rice
salt
about 3 tablespoons butter, cut into small pieces
oil or clarified butter

1 Wash the rice in a bowl, swishing through it with your hand, then drain off the water. Fill the bowl again and repeat the procedure about five or six times, until the water runs clear. Then fill the bowl with enough fresh water to cover the rice by about 2.5cm (1-inch); add 1 tablespoon salt, stir, and leave the rice to soak for at least 25 minutes.

2 In a large non-stick pan, bring 2–3 litres (70–105fl oz) water to the boil, then add 1 tablespoon salt. Drain the soaked rice in a sieve.

3 Pour the drained rice into the water at a rolling boil and cook briskly, uncovered, for around 4–7 minutes at a moderate-to-high heat, until it tests *al dente* (take out a grain of rice and press it between your fingers — you must still be able to feel a tiny, firm kernel). Drain the rice in a sieve.

4 Place the empty pan back onto a high heat. Pour in enough oil to cover the bottom of the pan, then add 80ml (3fl oz) of water and bring to the boil.

5 As soon as the water and oil mixture comes to the boil, spread the rice over the bottom of the pot with a slotted spoon, evenly at first, then loosely mounded up towards the centre. Dot evenly with the butter. Using the handle of a wooden spoon, make 5–8 holes in the rice that reach down to the bottom of the pan, allowing the steam to circulate fully.

6 As soon as the rice begins to steam (this should only take a few minutes), wrap the lid of the pot in a clean tea towel and place it tightly on top. This will allow the moisture to be collected in the cloth, leaving the rice dry. Only when the lid has become very hot on the outside (about 5 minutes) should the heat be reduced to the lowest possible setting. From now on, no matter how great the temptation, do not lift the lid again, as this will hinder the formation of the crispy crust on the bottom of the pan.

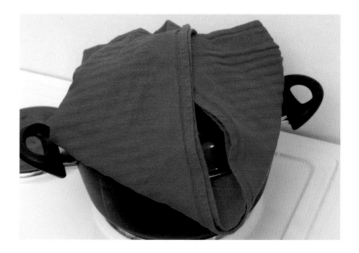

KATEH

STEAMED RICE

7 After about 60–70 minutes, the rice will be done. Remove the lid, and place a platter or large plate upside-down over the pan. Turn over the pan and the plate, giving them a gentle shake if necessary, so that the rice lands crust-side up on the plate, like a cake.

VARIATIONS FOR THE *TAHDIG* ('CRISPY BASE'):
- **For a saffron crust:** finely pound ¹/₂ teaspoon saffron threads in a mortar with a pinch of sugar. As soon as the oil and water mixture on the bottom of the pan has come to the boil, sprinkle in the saffron and stir with a wooden spoon. Spread the rice from the sieve on top, proceeding as described above.
- **For a potato crust:** peel and wash 1–2 potatoes and cut them into very thin slices. Spread the sliced potatoes side-by-side and close together in one layer on the bottom of the pan in the boiling oil and water mixture, season with salt, and pour the cooked rice from the sieve on top. Proceed as described above.
- **For a crunchy bread crust:** place 100g (3¹/₂oz) flour in a small bowl, add a generous pinch of salt and a pinch of sugar and mix. Add about 60ml (about 2fl oz) hot water, and knead to a soft, pliable dough (adding a little more water if necessary). Form the dough into a ball, cover in plastic wrap, and leave it to rest at room temperature for at least 15 minutes. While the rice is cooking to the *al dente* stage, roll out the dough thinly to the size of the pan base and place this circle of dough in the boiling oil and water mixture. Tip the rice on top, and proceed as described above.

TIP: Prepare the *tahdig* variant in advance, as the rice is soaking. If you are not using a non-stick pan, run 2–3cm (about 1-inch) of cold water into the sink just before the end of the cooking time, then take the covered pan straight from the heat and dip the base very briefly in the water: the *tahdig* will loosen from the bottom of the pan with a loud hiss, and you can now transfer the rice to a platter with a slotted spoon and lay the *tahdig*, whole, or broken into several pieces, on top of the rice, or serve it separately on a small plate.

SERVES 4
600g (1lb 5oz) basmati rice
1 litre (35fl oz) water
1 tablespoon salt
2 tablespoons butter

1 Before cooking, first wash the measured rice. To do this, pour it into a bowl, fill the bowl with lukewarm water, swish your hand around gently, and pour off the water, which will have gone cloudy with the loose starch. Repeat this process about five or six times, until the water finally runs clear.
2 Next, for each cup of rice, pour 2 cups of fresh water into a large non-stick pan, and add salt. Pour in the drained rice and bring to the boil, uncovered, over a high heat. Skim off any scum with a slotted spoon.
3 When the water just covers the rice and no more, add the butter and wait until the water has been almost completely absorbed – but no longer – as the rice must still be quite moist.
4 Wrap the lid in a tea towel and place tightly on the pan. Reduce the heat to a low setting and let the rice steam for 45 minutes.

TIP: The degree of separation of the rice grains depends on the quantity of water used in cooking, as well as the variety and age of the rice. For drier, fluffier rice, use just one cup of water for every cup of rice. Those who cook Persian rice fairly often may also wish to buy an electric rice cooker, which makes it easy to produce perfect rice. Ask for advice in a Persian shop, and note that Chinese or Thai rice cookers are not suitable for Persian rice, where you are looking to create a crust.

NOTE: With *kateh*, the water is not poured off after the first stage of cooking. As a result, the rice does not turn out quite as fluffy as with the *chelo* process. The positive advantage to this is that the valuable nutrients present in hulled white rice will not be discarded with the water.

ZERESHK POLO BA MORGH

SAFFRON RICE WITH CHICKEN AND BARBERRIES

SERVES 4

FOR THE CHICKEN:

1 chicken (or 4 large chicken legs)

salt, pepper

1 large onion

1 teaspoon turmeric

1/2 teaspoon saffron, ground

2–3 bay leaves

groundnut or maize-germ oil

FOR THE BARBERRIES:

250g (9oz) barberries

2 tablespoons clarified butter (or 1 tablespoon oil and
1 tablespoon butter)

2–3 tablespoons brown sugar

1/4 teaspoon cinnamon

YOU WILL ALSO NEED:

4 servings of *chelo*, *see* recipe page 72

1/4 teaspoon saffron, ground

1 Wash the rice and soak for at least 25 minutes.

2 Wash and cut up the chicken, separating the thigh
and drumstick pieces at the joint. Season the chicken
portions with salt and pepper, and refrigerate while the
rice is soaking.

3 At the end of the soaking time, set the rice on to cook.
As soon as it is steaming in the pot (at the 'second stage'
of cooking), peel and quarter the onion. Heat the oil in
a large, deep pan and stir-fry the onion pieces for about
3 minutes, until golden. Sprinkle with turmeric and place
the chicken portions on top. Sprinkle the chicken with
the saffron, add the bay leaves and cover with the lid.
Let everything sear well for about 5 minutes.

4 Meanwhile, boil some water and pour 150ml (5fl oz)
over the chicken, then reduce the heat to low.
Gently braise the chicken, covered, for a good hour, until
the rice is also done.

5 While the chicken is braising and the rice is steaming,
pour the barberries onto a flat plate and sort through
them, removing any tiny stones. Rinse the berries in a
sieve with cold water and drain them well.

6 About 15 minutes before the rice and chicken are done,
heat the clarified butter (or the oil-and-butter mixture)
in a small pan over a medium heat. Add the drained
barberries to the hot fat and stir once. Sprinkle on the
sugar and stir briefly until it caramelizes slightly, keeping
the heat at a moderate setting to prevent the berries from
turning black. De-glaze with 3 tablespoons chicken broth
from the braising pan and add the cinnamon; turn the
heat up to its maximum setting and continue stirring for
1–2 minutes. Take the barberries off the heat and set aside,
covered, until needed (you may need to reheat briefly
before serving).

7 Shortly before serving, place the ground saffron in a
small bowl and dissolve in about 60ml (2fl oz) boiling
water. Add a ladleful of rice from the pot, and carefully
mix with the dissolved saffron.

8 Serve the rice separately from the crust – heap the white
rice onto a large tray and garnish with the saffron rice.
Distribute the barberries decoratively over the top
(or hand around separately in a small bowl, if you prefer).
Serve the rice crust separately on a plate, whole or broken
into several large pieces.

9 The chicken pieces can either be served directly from
the braising pan with the rice, or can be arranged with
the rice.

TIP: Finely chop a handful of pistachios and sprinkle these
over the rice; this makes for a particularly beautiful colour
combination in this classic Persian dish.

Following pages: Decked out in pink tulle,
the bride takes centre position in a
group of brightly dressed women.

SABZI POLO

HERBED RICE

SERVES 4

450g (1lb) basmati rice

oil

large bunches (sufficient to fill one good cup when
  chopped) fresh herbs (chives, parsley, coriander in
  about equal proportions)

1 garlic bulb

salt

1/2 teaspoon saffron, ground

1/4 teaspoon cinnamon

1 Wash the rice in several changes of water and soak in
cold water with 1 teaspoon salt for at least 25 minutes.

2 Meanwhile, wash and shake dry the herbs and remove
the stalks. Peel the garlic and chop it very finely together
with the herbs.

3 Bring 2–3 litres (70–105fl oz) water to the boil in a
large non-stick pan and add 1 tablespoon salt. Pour the
drained rice into the boiling water and cook at a rolling
boil for about 3–7 minutes. As soon as the rice tests *al
dente*, add the herbs and garlic and stir once, so that
everything is well mixed.

4 Drain the herbed rice in a sieve, shaking the sieve a few
times to remove as much water as possible.

5 Place the pan back on the stove (on a moderate setting)
and add enough oil to cover the bottom of the pan
completely. Add 80ml (about 3fl oz) water. As soon as the
oil-and-water mixture comes to the boil, stir in half the
saffron and season with salt. With a slotted spoon,
distribute some of the herbed rice in the pan so that the
bottom is well covered.

6 Add the remaining rice, mounding it up loosely towards
the centre of the pot. Sprinkle the rice with cinnamon and
evenly pour over 1–2 tablespoons of oil (or dot with a little
butter) and a further 40ml (about 1 1/2fl oz) water. With
the handle of a wooden spoon, make five holes in the
mound of rice that reach down to the bottom of the pan.

7 As soon as the rice begins to steam (about 5–10 minutes), wrap the lid in a tea towel and place tightly on the
pan (resisting all temptations to lift it again) and lower the
heat to the lowest setting. After about 70–80 minutes,

the rice will be done, and you will have a crunchy, golden-
brown rice crust (*tahdig*) on the bottom of the pan.

8 Just before serving, dissolve the remaining saffron in a
small bowl in a scant 40ml (about 1 1/2fl oz) hot water.
Skim off a ladleful of rice and mix – carefully, so that the
rice grains remain intact – with the dissolved saffron.

9 Place a large platter upside-down on top of the pan.
Gently turn over the pan and the plate, shaking carefully if
necessary, so that the rice lands crust-side up, like a cake.

10 Serve the rice crust separately, broken into several
large pieces. Use the saffron rice to decorate the dish.

NOTE: *Sabzi polo* has many variations, and can be combined in a variety of ways. As a traditional dish at *Noruz*,
the Persian New Year, it is served with fish pan-fried in a
little butter, and herb *kuku* (*see* recipe page 44).

TIP: For *Sabzi polo ba mahi* (Herbed rice with fish), you
will need 1kg (2 1/4lb) whole, gutted white fish with its
head and tail (or 4 good-sized fillets from a firm-fleshed
fish such as carp). Cut the fish into small chunks and
season with salt. Gently fry in butter (with a few whole
garlic cloves if liked) and serve with fresh lemon wedges
along with the rice

Right: The house of the prosperous Borujerdi merchant
family in Kashan is decorated with sumptuous murals.

KALAM POLO
RICE WITH WHITE CABBAGE

SERVES 4

450g (1lb) basmati rice
salt, pepper
2 onions
500g (1lb 4oz) minced (ground) beef
oil
1 teaspoon saffron, ground
500g (1lb 2oz) white cabbage, sliced into thin strips
1 teaspoon turmeric

1 Wash the rice in several changes of water and drain. Soak for about 1 hour in cold water to which 2 tablespoons of salt have been added.

2 While the rice is soaking, finely grate one of the onions and mix with the minced beef and a generous pinch of ground saffron; season with salt and pepper. Knead everything well with your hands until you have an even mixture.

3 Roll the meat mixture between your palms into table-tennis-sized balls, moistening your hands from time to time in a bowl of water.

4 Pan-fry the meatballs in a little oil until browned all over; lift out of the pan and drain on a plate lined with paper towel.

5 Heat a little oil in a large non-stick pan over a medium-to-high flame. Add the cabbage and fry until translucent and slightly golden, then drain on a plate lined with paper towels.

6 Finely chop the remaining onion and fry in a little oil, in the same pan you used to sauté the cabbage, until golden. Sprinkle with turmeric and stir twice. Add the cabbage and mix with the onion; lower the heat. Place the meatballs on top, season with pepper, a generous pinch of ground saffron and a little salt. Carefully mix all the ingredients and turn off the heat, leaving the meatballs covered in the pan until needed.

7 Bring about 2 litres (70fl oz) water to the boil in a large non-stick pan. Add the drained rice and cook for 4–6 minutes at a rolling boil until it tests *al dente*. Drain in a sieve, and turn the heat to medium.

8 Place the empty pan back on the heat and add sufficient oil to completely cover the bottom of the pan. Add 125ml (4fl oz) water. As soon as it comes to the boil, sprinkle the remaining saffron into the oil and water mixture.

9 With a skimmer, transfer some of the rice from the sieve into the pan, spreading it evenly over the bottom. Spread part of the meat, cabbage and onion mixture over the rice and cover with a layer of rice. Cover with another layer of the meat mixture, continuing to alternate the layers until the pan is full. The rice should be piled up towards the centre of the pan. Sprinkle 1 teaspoon cinnamon over the rice. With the handle of a wooden spoon, make five holes in the mound of rice that reach right down to the bottom of the pan.

10 As soon as the rice begins to steam (about 5–10 minutes), wrap the lid in a tea towel and place tightly on the pan, resisting all temptation to lift the lid from this point on. Reduce the heat to the minimum setting.

11 After 70–80 minutes, the dish will be done and a rice crust will have formed on the bottom of the pan. Remove the lid, and place a large plate upside-down over the pan. Turn the pan over, keeping the plate in place and shaking gently so that the rice lands on the plate crust-side up.

VARIATION: A rather more exotic-tasting *kalam polo* is prepared in Shiraz. For this recipe, you will also need:

50g (1³/₄oz) each fresh dill, parsley,
wild garlic and basil
150ml (5fl oz) pomegranate syrup
1–2 teaspoons black cumin

1 Wash the herbs, remove their stalks and finely chop the leaves.

2 Prepare the meat mixture as described above; form into balls and brown. Add the pomegranate syrup, stir, and turn off the heat, leaving the meatballs in the pan.

3 Fry the cabbage as described above and season with the cumin.

4 Boil the rice. Just before draining it, add the chopped herbs to the cooking water, stir, and drain in a sieve.

5 Arrange the rice, cabbage and meatballs in alternating layers and steam as above.

Left: The butchers' shops in any Iranian bazaar are grouped together along a single long passage.

BAQALI POLO BA GUSHT

DILLED RICE WITH BROAD (FAVA) BEANS AND VEAL

SERVES 4

FOR THE MEAT:

1 large onion

oil

1 teaspoon turmeric

1kg (2¼lb) veal with bone (shoulder)

5 garlic cloves

½ teaspoon saffron, ground

1 pinch cinnamon

2 bay leaves

salt, pepper

FOR THE RICE:

450g (1lb) basmati rice

salt

60g (2¼oz) dried dill tips

180g (6¼oz) dried broad (fava) beans (*baqali*), sorted
   through and soaked overnight

1 teaspoon saffron, ground

1 tablespoon butter

2 large potatoes, peeled and cut into thin slices

oil

1 First get the meat underway: peel the onion, halve it
lengthways, and slice thinly. Heat a little oil in a large pan
and fry the onion until golden. Sprinkle on the turmeric
and stir.

2 Add the meat and fry for 5 minutes, stirring. Pour in
sufficient hot water to just cover the meat and add the
garlic cloves to the pan. Bring everything to the boil.
Add ¼ teaspoon saffron, the cinnamon and the bay leaves.
Season with salt and pepper. Reduce the heat, cover, and
simmer the meat for at least 1½ hours (*see* Tip).

3 While the meat is braising, prepare the dilled rice with
broad beans. Wash the rice and soak in cold water with
1 tablespoon salt for 25 minutes. Weigh the dill and set
aside in a small bowl. Drain the beans and rinse with
fresh water.

4 Take a large non-stick pan, put the beans in 2–3 litres
(70–105fl oz) water and bring to the boil. Boil the beans
briskly for 20–30 minutes; at this point they should be
cooked, but still retain some 'bite'. Skim off any scum.

5 In a small bowl, pour 40ml (1½fl oz) boiling water
over ½ teaspoon saffron. Add 1 tablespoon butter, cover,
and set aside.

6 Drain the soaked rice in a sieve. Add to the beans (still
on the heat), stir, and cook for 4–7 minutes at a rolling
boil, until the rice tests *al dente*.

7 Drain the rice and bean mixture in a sieve and set the
hotplate to a medium heat.

8 Place the empty pan back on the heat and pour in
sufficient oil to completely cover the bottom of the pan.
Add 80ml (about 2½fl oz) hot water; sprinkle ½ teaspoon
saffron into the oil and water mixture and stir. Place the
sliced potatoes in a single layer on the bottom of the pan
and season with salt.

9 Pour about one-third of the rice and bean mixture from
the sieve onto the potato slices; scatter half the dill in a
layer on top, followed by another layer of rice and beans.
Sprinkle the remaining dill over the top and finish with
the last of the rice and bean mixture. The rice should be
piled up towards the centre.

10 Using the handle of a wooden spoon, make 5 holes in
the rice that reach down as far as the potato layer. Pour the
reserved saffron water over the rice.

11 Wrap the lid of the pan in a tea towel and place it
tightly on top (resisting the temptation to lift the lid
from this point on). As soon as the lid is hot on the outside
(about 5 minutes), set the heat to low. After 70–80 minutes the rice will be done and a crunchy potato crust will
have formed on the bottom.

12 To serve, dissolve the remaining ¼ teaspoon saffron in
4 tablespoons veal stock from the pan, and distribute over
the rice. Serve with the meat and sauce.

TIP: A pressure cooker is ideal for preparing the meat;
cooking time is significantly reduced (always follow the
manufacturer's instructions), and all the flavours are sealed
in beautifully.

ADAS POLO
LENTIL RICE WITH DATES

SERVES 4

450g (1lb) basmati rice

salt, pepper

200g (7oz) *adas* (lentils that are relatively firm to the bite; black caviar or green Puy lentils are ideal)

1 large onion

oil

1 teaspoon turmeric

10 dates, stoned and quartered

50g (1³/₄oz) sultanas (optional)

¹/₄–¹/₂ teaspoon cinnamon, according to taste

¹/₂ teaspoon saffron, ground

1–2 tablespoons butter (or clarified butter)

1 teaspoon black cumin (optional; *see* Tip)

YOU WILL ALSO NEED:

5 tablespoons yogurt (or more, to taste)

1 Wash the rice in several changes of water, drain, and soak in cold water with 2 tablespoons salt for about 1 hour.

2 Sort through and wash the lentils, and boil them until they are *al dente* (cooking times depend upon the variety, so read the package). Drain in a sieve, then season with salt and pepper.

3 Finely chop the onion. Heat some oil in a large pan and fry the onion until soft and golden. Sprinkle with turmeric and stir once.

4 Add the dates and continue frying the mixture for around 3–4 minutes.

5 If using sultanas, add them to the onion and date mixture and stir two or three times. Sprinkle evenly with the cinnamon and half the saffron.

6 Tip the drained lentils into the pan, stirring everything carefully to combine. Remove from the heat.

7 Bring 2–3 litres (70–105fl oz) water to the boil in a large non-stick pan, then add 1 tablespoon salt. Drain the rice in a sieve and tip into the boiling water. Cook at a rolling boil for 4–6 minutes, until it tests *al dente*. Turn the heat to medium.

8 Drain the rice again, and carefully mix in the sieve with 1 tablespoon butter (or clarified butter), taking care not to damage the rice grains.

9 Place the empty pan back on the heat and pour in sufficient oil to cover the bottom of the pan; add 80ml (about 3fl oz) water. As soon as the water and oil mixture boils, sprinkle in the remaining saffron and stir.

10 With a skimmer, remove the rice from the sieve, spreading some of it evenly over the bottom of the pan. Spread part of the lentil mixture over the top, then follow with another layer of rice. Continue building up alternate layers of rice and lentils until the pan is full. The contents of the pan should be piled up towards the centre (most easily done by carefully running a wooden spoon around the outer edge). With the handle of the wooden spoon, make five holes in the rice that reach right down to the bottom of the pan.

11 As soon as the rice begins to steam (about 5–10 minutes), wrap the lid in a cloth and place it tightly on the pan, resisting any temptation to lift it again from this point on. Reduce the heat to low and steam the rice for about 70–80 minutes, until done.

12 To serve, remove the lid and place a large plate upside-down over the pan. Turn the pan over, keeping the plate in place, and shake carefully, so that the rice lands crust-side-up on the plate, like a cake. Hand round the yogurt separately.

TIP: Black cumin (*Bunium persicum*), or *zireh* in Parsi, a plant species from the numerous caraway family, goes very well with this dish. Use about 1 teaspoon of cumin in total, and sprinkle the seeds over the individual layers to make this dish particularly fragrant. *Zireh* also tones down the flatulent effect of the lentils and calms the stomach — so give it a try!

Following pages: Yazd lies along the Silk Road, between Isfahan and Kerman. The famous wind towers have been built for centuries to give 'natural' air conditioning, and help make the sweltering summers bearable.

ALBALU POLO
SOUR-CHERRY RICE

SERVES 4

450g (1lb) basmati rice
salt, pepper
2 medium onions
1 teaspoon turmeric
400g (1lb) lamb (shoulder), cut into large cubes
½ teaspoon saffron, ground
1 jar candied morello cherries (400g/1lb drained weight)
2–3 tablespoons sugar (optional)
groundnut oil or clarified butter
½ teaspoon cinnamon

1 Wash the rice, cover generously with lukewarm water to which 2 tablespoons salt have been added, and soak for about 1 hour.

2 Finely chop the onions and fry them in a large pan in a little oil until golden. Add the turmeric and lamb and fry for 5–6 minutes.

3 Add about 500ml (18fl oz) boiling water to the meat and simmer, covered, over a low heat for 1 hour. Not less than 15 minutes before the end of the cooking time, add a generous pinch of saffron, salt and pepper. Remove the lid and simmer for a further 5–8 minutes, so that no more than a good 225ml (4fl oz) of liquid remains at the end.

4 While the meat is cooking, simmer the cherries, uncovered, in a small saucepan (adding the sugar if they taste sharp) for 10–15 minutes, then set aside.

5 Bring 2 litres (70fl oz) water to the boil in a large non-stick pan. Drain the rice, add it to the pan together with 1 teaspoon salt, and cook at a rolling boil for 4–7 minutes, until the rice tests *al dente*. Turn the heat to a medium setting.

6 Drain the rice again and carefully mix it in the sieve with a little clarified butter, taking care not to damage the grains. Place the empty pan back on the heat and add sufficient oil to completely cover the bottom of the pan. Add 60ml (2¼fl oz) water, and as soon as it boils, sprinkle the remaining saffron into the oil and water mixture and stir once.

7 Using a skimmer, spread some of the sieved rice evenly over the bottom of the pan.

8 Place a little meat and a few cherries on top of the rice, using the skimmer. Cover this layer with rice. Continue building up alternate loose layers of meat, cherries, and rice until the pan is full. The contents of the pan should be piled up towards the centre.

9 With the handle of a wooden spoon, make five holes in the rice that reach down to the bottom of the pan. Sprinkle the top with cinnamon.

10 As soon as the rice begins to steam (about 5–10 minutes), wrap the lid in a tea towel, place it tightly onto the pan (resisting the temptation to lift the lid again from this point on), and reduce the heat to the lowest setting.

11 After about 70–80 minutes the dish will be ready and a rice crust will have formed on the bottom of the pan. Remove the lid and place a large plate upside-down over the pan. Turn the pan over, keeping the plate in place, and shake carefully, so that the rice lands crust-side up on the plate, like a cake.

NOTE: *Albalu polo* is a particularly festive sweet-savoury rice dish, often served at large parties.

Right: The salt is taken away from the *Namak* Lake in the Kavir Desert in large lorries.

SHIRIN POLO

SWEET RICE WITH CHICKEN, PISTACHIOS AND BITTER ORANGES

SERVES 4

450g (1lb) basmati rice

salt, pepper

1 chicken (or 4 large legs)

1–2 large onions (according to taste)

1 teaspoon turmeric

1 teaspoon saffron, ground

6 tablespoons brown sugar

about 2 handfuls untreated (bitter-) orange peel, cut into
    fine strips (or 1 handful dried bitter-orange peel, available
    in Persian shops)

3 carrots

2–3 tablespoons butter

1 handful pistachios, chopped, or almonds, flaked (or a
    mixture of both)

1 handful sultanas

clarified butter

oil

1 Wash the rice in several changes of water, drain, and
soak for about 1 hour in cold water to which 2 tablespoons
salt have been added.

2 Wash and cut up the meat. If using a whole chicken,
remove and quarter the breast. Cut through the legs at
the joint. (The carcass and wings can be saved for making
stock or soup.)

3 Quarter the onion(s). Heat a little oil in a large pan
and sear the onion pieces for 2 minutes, then sprinkle with
the turmeric.

4 Lay the chicken pieces on the onions, sprinkle with
salt, pepper and a little of the saffron, and pour in 60ml
(2¼fl oz) water. Reduce the heat to low and braise gently
with the lid on for 1½ hours. (Keep topping up with a
little boiling water whenever necessary; the bottom of the
pan must not be allowed to dry out, and should still have a
thin covering of liquid at the end of the cooking time.)

5 Meanwhile, in a small saucepan, bring 250ml (9fl oz)
water to the boil. Dissolve 4 tablespoons brown sugar in
the boiling water; add the bitter-orange peel and boil for 6
minutes, then set aside.

6 Peel the carrots and cut diagonally into thin slices. Melt
the butter in a non-stick pan. Add the carrots along with
the remaining sugar, and caramelize over a low heat. Care
needs to be taken at this stage, as it takes a while for the
sugar to begin to caramelize, but it will then burn quite
quickly. The sugar should turn golden-brown.

7 Add the nuts, sultanas and the drained orange peel, stir,
and remove the pan from the heat.

8 Bring 2–3 litres (70–105fl oz) water to the boil in a
large, non-stick pan; add 1 tablespoon salt and the drained
rice. Cook the rice at a fast boil over a medium-to-high
heat for 4–7 minutes, until it tests al dente. Drain, then
mix carefully in the sieve with a little clarified butter,
taking care not to damage the grains.

9 Put the pan back on the heat, pour in enough oil to
completely cover the bottom of the pan, then add 80ml
(about 3fl oz) hot water. As soon as the oil and water
mixture comes to the boil, sprinkle in about ¾ teaspoon
ground saffron and stir.

10 Using a skimmer, evenly spread a layer of rice over the
bottom of the pan. Top with a little of the carrot mixture,
then loosely layer some more rice on top. Carry on building up alternate layers of rice and carrot until you have
used them all up. The contents of the pan should be piled
up towards the centre (use a wooden spoon to coax the
ingredients into the right shape).

11 With the handle of the wooden spoon, make five holes
in the rice that reach down to the bottom of the pan.

12 Wrap the lid in a tea towel and place it tightly on the
pan, resisting the temptation to lift it again from this
point on. Reduce the heat to the lowest setting, and steam
the rice for about 80–90 minutes. The rice will then be
done, and a golden-brown crust will have formed on the
bottom of the pan.

13 Just before the end of the cooking time, dissolve the
remaining ¼ teaspoon saffron in 3 tablespoons boiling
water. Carefully mix with a ladleful of rice.

14 To serve, arrange the rice on a large platter and lay the
chicken pieces on top. Decorate with the saffron rice.
Hand round the sauce and the tahdig separately.

NOTE: Shirin polo is a very special festive dish that is
served on special occasions. The fruity-sweet taste of
the polo harmonizes perfectly with the braised chicken.
If you have never tried shirin polo, then your knowledge of
Persian cuisine is not yet complete!

PESTEH POLO BA GUSHT

PISTACHIO RICE WITH LAMB

SERVES 4

FOR THE PISTACHIO RICE:

450g (1lb) rice

large bunch (sufficient to make half a cup when chopped)
  fresh dill

200–300g (7–10^{1}/$_{2}$oz) pistachios, shelled and halved
  (or flaked)

oil

^{3}/$_{4}$ teaspoon saffron, ground

1 teaspoon butter, plus a little extra, cut into small pieces

salt

FOR THE MEAT:

1 large onion

oil

1 teaspoon turmeric

1kg (2lb 4oz) lamb, cut into large cubes

2 bay leaves

salt, coarsely ground pepper

^{1}/$_{2}$ teaspoon saffron, ground

1 Wash the rice and soak for about 1 hour in cold water
to which 1 tablespoon salt has been added.

2 While the rice is soaking, wash the dill, remove the
stalks and chop the leaves finely. Keep cool until needed.

3 To start the meat dish, cut the onion into quarters.
Heat some oil in a large pan and sear the onion pieces
briefly over a high heat, then sprinkle over the turmeric.
Add the meat, and brown briefly on all sides.

4 Add the bay leaves and pepper and pour 160ml
(5^{1}/$_{2}$fl oz) boiling water over the meat. Reduce the heat to
low and gently simmer the meat, covered, for 1 hour. If
too much liquid has evaporated and the ingredients seem
likely to burn, add boiling water a large spoonful at a
time. There should always be a small amount of liquid on
the bottom of the pan.

5 Now add the saffron to the meat, season with salt, and
braise at the lowest setting until the rice is also done.

6 For the rice, bring 2–3 litres (70–105fl oz) water to
the boil in a large non-stick pan. Tip in the drained rice,
and boil briskly for 4–6 minutes, until *al dente*. Add the
pistachios and dill, stir once, and cook for just 1 more
minute (the rice must still have some 'bite'). Then drain
everything through a sieve, shaking carefully. Set the heat
to moderate.

7 Place the pan back on the heat. Pour in enough oil to
completely cover the bottom of the pan, then add 80ml
(about 3fl oz) water.

8 As soon as the oil and water mixture comes to a boil,
sprinkle in ^{1}/$_{4}$ teaspoon saffron, stir, and season with salt.
Place a good layer of the rice mixture onto the bottom of
the pan. Top loosely with the remaining rice mixture,
piling it up towards the centre.

9 Melt the butter in 40ml (1^{1}/$_{2}$fl oz) boiling water and
pour over the rice. With the handle of a wooden spoon,
make five holes in the rice that reach down to the bottom
of the pan. Dot the top with a little extra butter.

10 As soon as the rice begins to steam (about 5–10
minutes), wrap the lid in a cloth and place it tightly on
the pan, resisting the temptation to lift it again from this
point on. Reduce the heat to the lowest setting. After
80–90 minutes, the rice will be done and the rice crust
(*tahdig*) will have formed on the bottom.

11 To serve, dissolve the remaining saffron in about
40ml (1^{1}/$_{2}$fl oz) boiling water and 2 tablespoons of the
meat stock, and pour evenly over the rice. Arrange the
meat and rice on a platter, and hand round the sauce and
the rice crust – broken into pieces – separately as an
accompaniment.

TIP: This delicate dish is also excellent prepared with a large,
fresh chicken instead of the lamb. Use a whole chicken,
removing the legs first, then halving them again at the joint.
Cut the breast and back in half, then remove the breast meat
from the bone and cut into four small pieces. The wings and
carcass can be reserved to make stock or soup. The ingredients are the same as for the recipe with lamb, but omit the
bay leaves and use just ^{1}/$_{2}$ teaspoon turmeric instead of
1 teaspoon. Heat a little oil in a deep pan and sear the onions
for about 3 minutes at maximum heat. Now sprinkle over
the turmeric, place the chicken pieces in the pan, and sprinkle the chicken with the saffron. Cover and sear over a high
heat for about 5 minutes. Now deglaze the pan with 160ml
(about 5^{1}/$_{2}$fl oz) boiling water, reduce to a low temperature,
and braise the chicken for about 1^{1}/$_{2}$–2 hours, until the rice
is also done.

NOTE: This dish was cooked back in Qajar times in Tehran,
but has largely faded into obscurity in the present day. It is
similar to *baqali polo*, but slightly more refined, primarily
because of the generous quantity of pistachios used.

TAH CHIN

RICE CAKE WITH CHICKEN AND YOGURT

SERVES 4

600g (1lb 5oz) basmati rice

salt

1 onion

1 large carrot

oil

1/2 teaspoon turmeric

2 chicken legs

1 1/2 teaspoons saffron, ground

2 bay leaves

2 eggs

1 tablespoon yogurt

1 teaspoon butter

1 Wash the rice in several changes of water, drain, and soak for about 1 hour in cold water to which 2 tablespoons salt have been added.

2 Quarter the onion. Wash and halve the carrot. Heat some oil in a large pan and sear the onion pieces over a high heat for about 3 minutes. Sprinkle with turmeric and place the chicken pieces on top. Sprinkle over 1/2 teaspoon saffron, add the carrot and bay leaves to the pan, cover, and fry everything for 5 minutes.

3 Pour in 150ml (5fl oz) boiling water, season with salt, cover, and braise over a low heat for a good 1 1/2 hours. Remove the chicken from the heat, leave to cool slightly, then bone the chicken and set aside.

4 Dissolve 1 teaspoon saffron in 40ml (1 1/2fl oz) boiling water in a small bowl and leave to cool.

5 Crack the eggs into a large bowl and beat hard with a fork. Stir in the yogurt and saffron water.

6 Bring 2–3 litres (70–105fl oz) water to the boil in a large non-stick pan. Add 1 teaspoon salt, tip in the drained rice and boil briskly over a moderate heat for 3–6 minutes, until it tests *al dente*. Drain well.

7 Place the empty pan back onto a low heat and add enough oil to cover the bottom of the pan. Increase the heat to moderate.

8 Mix half of the rice in the sieve with the egg and yogurt mixture in the bowl. Spread part of this mixture on the bottom of the pan to a depth of about 2.5cm (1-inch).

9 Layer the chicken on top of the rice and cover with the remaining rice mixture. Finally, top with the plain white rice. Bring everything to a high heat and cook for 5–10 minutes.

10 Meanwhile, dissolve the butter in about 80ml (2 1/2fl oz) boiling water. Pour the butter and water mixture evenly over the rice.

11 Wrap the lid in a tea towel, place it tightly on the pan, avoiding the temptation to lift it up again from this point on, and reduce to the lowest heat. The *tah chin* will be ready in about 80–90 minutes.

12 To serve, remove the lid and place a platter or large plate upside-down over the pan. Turn over the pan and the plate, giving them a gentle shake if necessary, so that the rice lands crust-side up on the plate, like a cake. Serve the rice cut into wedges.

NOTE: Eggs and yogurt create a shiny and very crunchy golden crust. This rice dish is particularly attractive served like a cake, cut into slices.

Right: Detail of the tilework in Tehran's *Golestan* Palace.

BRAISED DISHES

KHORESH, KHORAK AND ABGUSHT

Next to rice, *khoresh* is the most important component of Persian cuisine, and is always served with rice (*chelo* or *kateh*). It is the main daily meal of most Iranians. Regardless of the occasion, every Persian meal contains at least one *khoresh* with *chelo* as a main dish.

A *khoresh* always consists of a mixture of meat and various vegetables and fruits, cooked over a fairly long time, melding into a highly aromatic sauce. The time the rice takes to cook (about 1½ hours) should always be included in the preparation. The meat used for *khoresh* should be a cut of lamb; lamb shoulder is recommended, as it is flavourful and delicate, but leg of lamb, or even veal or beef, are also suitable meats.

Long and gentle cooking over a low heat allows the flavours of the ingredients of a *khoresh* to develop fully and mix together completely. Most *khoresh* will even improve if they are prepared a day in advance and reheated before serving (an exception being *Khoresht-e fesenjan*, Duck with walnuts). A *khoresh* should be thick in consistency, and in any case never so wet that the ingredients sink or even swim in the liquid – after all, this is not a soup! Salt and acidifiers are only added to the *khoresh* at the end – otherwise, the meat and pulses will take longer to cook. Cinnamon and saffron should also only be added towards the end of the cooking time, as the taste of these spices will otherwise fade.

In addition to *chelo*, the usual accompaniments served with *khoresh* are *torshi* (sour, pickled vegetables), yogurt or variations on a yogurt theme, and of course fresh herbs, including flat-leaf parsley, chives, dill, fresh mint, Thai basil and wild garlic, as well as radishes and spring onions. Unlike *khoresh*, *khorak* is served with bread instead of rice. Otherwise the cooking methods are similar.

One of the most typical and traditional dishes of Persian cuisine, *abgusht* is difficult to find outside Iran. Literally translated, *abgusht* means 'water-meat'.

Abgusht actually consists of a strong meat stock cooked from various ingredients. Its secret, however, lies in the last step of its preparation, and the way in which it is served and eaten. It consists of two courses, *teride abgusht* and *gusht-e kubideh*: *gusht-e kubideh* ('pounded meat') is the meat itself which, at the end of the cooking time, just before eating, is removed from the stock and pounded together with the accompaniments using a large, flattened pestle. *Teride abgusht* (literally 'meat-and-water mixture') is effectively the soup, and consists of the meat stock in which bread is dunked. Despite its name, *abgusht* consists not only of meat and water, but of numerous other ingredients, such as pulses, herbs, *kashk*, vegetables, dried fruits, pomegranate juice, walnuts, and many more.

The meat for *abgusht* is usually cooked with the bone, since this gives the stock a good consistency and fine flavour. *Abgusht* has a reddish hue, achieved by a combination of saffron, turmeric and tomatoes. The delicately tart taste comes from the dried limes (*limu omani*), unripe grapes, or prunes. *Abgusht* is served with raw onions, *torshi* (sour pickled vegetables), fresh herbs, radishes, and always with bread. In Iran, this is a special bread (*nan-e sangak*) baked on pebbles, but pitta bread or Indian nan bread can be served equally well.

Abgusht is an undemanding dish as, once the soup is cooking, it can simmer unattended for a long time. What's more, although the ingredients may be simple, an excellent taste is guaranteed – just as with any honest meat stock, except that here the taste is more refined.

Abgusht is currently undergoing a real renaissance: restaurants in Tehran now offer it, prepared with great skill and panache in a traditional atmosphere, and the city's inhabitants are coming to realize that this dish is one of the most brilliant and enduring creations in the long history of Near Eastern cuisine.

Right: Abgusht is traditionally served in tall vessels made from metal, clay or wood.

KHORESHT-E BADEMJAN
AUBERGINE (EGGPLANT) AND LAMB STEW

SERVES 4

5 aubergines (eggplants), about 1kg/2¼lb

salt, pepper

oil

1 large onion

1 teaspoon turmeric

500g (1lb 2oz) shoulder of lamb (boned)

¼ teaspoon saffron, ground

5 firm tomatoes (or 1 tablespoon tomato paste)

2–3 tablespoons verjuice (available in good delicatessens or in some supermarkets), or 3–4 tablespoons freshly squeezed lemon juice

YOU WILL ALSO NEED:

4 servings of rice (*chelo*), *see* recipe page 72

1 Wash the rice in several changes of water, drain, and leave to soak in cold water to which 1 tablespoon salt has been added.

2 Peel the aubergines and halve them lengthways. Make a lengthways slit in the centre of each half with a knife. Carefully salt all the halves and place them side-by-side on paper towels to drain for at least 2 hours. Cut the aubergines into small cubes.

3 Heat sufficient oil in a non-stick pan to cover the bottom of the pan by a good 1cm (½-inch). Carefully pat the aubergines dry and fry in batches on both sides until brown. Set aside.

4 Finely chop the onion. Heat a little oil in a large pan, and fry the onion over a medium heat until golden. Sprinkle over the turmeric and stir once.

5 Cut the lamb into cubes and add to the onions. Fry for 8–10 minutes, until lightly browned. Sprinkle the saffron over the meat, season with pepper, and stir once.

6 Finely chop 4 of the 5 tomatoes and add to the pan with the meat. Simmer over a low heat for 10 minutes, stirring several times, until the tomato sauce thickens and turns dark red. (If you cannot get hold of any flavourful fresh tomatoes, use 1 tablespoon tomato paste instead: add the tomato paste to the meat and cook for just 3–4 minutes, until the colour grows darker and the tomato fragrance

begins to rise.)

7 Pour 250ml (9fl oz) boiling water over the meat and the thickened sauce and bring everything to a boil, then reduce heat to low, cover firmly, and simmer for about 1½ hours. Top up the liquid in the pan with a little boiling water as often as necessary. In principle, however, the less water that evaporates and has therefore to be replaced, the better. Flavour escapes along with the steam, and the *khoresh* is meant to be thick.

8 After the meat has been cooking for 1 hour, season to taste with salt, stir, and continue simmering. While the meat simmers, put on the rice for *chelo* (see page 72).

9 As soon as the rice is steaming in the pan, place the aubergine slices on the meat (do not stir from this point on). There should be enough liquid in the pan to just cover the aubergines. Cut the remaining tomato into slices and place on top of the aubergine. Cover, and braise gently over a low heat for a further 30 minutes.

10 Next, gently push the layered *khoresh* to one side with a spoon in a single spot, and pour in the verjuice (or lemon juice). Carefully lift the pan off the heat and tilt it carefully in all directions to distribute the juice evenly. Take care not to damage the aubergine-and-tomato layer while doing this.

11 Replace the pan on the heat. Sprinkle the tomatoes with cinnamon, cover, and simmer everything for a further 30 minutes or so. Serve with the rice.

VARIATIONS: For *khoresht-e kadu va bademjan* (with courgettes/zucchini), replace half the aubergines with courgettes; the initial and subsequent preparation of the courgettes is the same as that described for aubergines.

For *khoresht-e bamieh* (with okra), replace half the aubergines with young, fresh okra pods. Wash and trim the okra pods before cooking, taking care to leave them intact; otherwise, the viscous liquid exuded by the okra during cooking will spoil the consistency of the finished dish. Fry the okra in a little oil over a medium heat for 10–12 minutes, until golden, then layer them over the browned meat and proceed as described in the recipe.

Right: Scene in the Kashan bazaar.

KHORESHT-E QEYMEH
LAMB STEW WITH LIMES

SERVES 4

80g (2³/₄oz) *lapeh* (yellow lentils)

4 firm tomatoes (or 1 tablespoon tomato paste)

1 medium onion

oil

1 teaspoon turmeric

500g (1lb 2oz) lamb (boned leg), cut into small cubes

salt, pepper

¹/₂ teaspoon saffron, ground

2 bay leaves

2–3 *limu omani* (dried limes)

3–4 medium potatoes

YOU WILL ALSO NEED:

4 servings of rice (*chelo*), *see* recipe page 72

1 The day before you want to cook the dish, sort through the *lapeh* (yellow lentils), pour over boiling water to cover, and leave to soak overnight. The next day, drain the lentils in a sieve and rinse with fresh water.

2 Coarsely grate the tomatoes and set aside.

3 Finely chop the onion. Heat some oil in a large pan and fry the onion until golden. Sprinkle with turmeric and stir once.

4 Add the cubed lamb and fry for 8–10 minutes, until light brown on all sides. Sprinkle with pepper and saffron, add the bay leaves, and fry for a further 2–3 minutes, stirring constantly.

5 Add the grated tomatoes to the meat, cover, and simmer over a very low heat for 10 minutes, stirring occasionally, until the tomato sauce thickens. (If you cannot get hold of any flavourful tomatoes, use 1 tablespoon tomato paste instead. Add the tomato paste to the meat and fry for just 3–4 minutes or so, until the colour darkens and the fragrance of the tomato paste rises.)

6 Pour over 250ml (9fl oz) boiling water and bring everything to the boil over a high heat.

7 Prick the limes in several places with a fork to prevent them exploding while cooking, and place in the sauce with the lentils. If necessary, add just enough water to cover the lentils and meat by 1cm (¹/₂ inch) and bring to the boil. Reduce heat to low, cover the pan, and simmer for at least 1¹/₂ hours. If the level of liquid in the pan falls too low, top up with a little boiling water as necessary. In principle, however, the less water that evaporates and has to be replaced, the better. Flavour escapes with the steam, and the *khoresh* is meant to be thick. If, on the other hand, the stew becomes too thin, leave the lid open a crack.

8 While the meat simmers, prepare the rice for *chelo*: first wash the rice in several changes of water, drain, and soak for 25 minutes in lukewarm water to which 1 tablespoon salt has been added. Now continue as described on page 72, so that the rice and meat are ready at the same time.

9 About 20 minutes before the rice and meat are done, peel the potatoes and cut into matchsticks.

10 Heat a generous amount of oil in a large pan and fry the matchstick potatoes over a medium heat until crisp, then drain on paper towel.

11 Serve the stew, topped with the crisp-fried matchstick potatoes, with the rice.

TIP: The crisp potatoes are an essential part of this dish. If need be, you could always resort to takeout fries, but of course the taste cannot compare to the homemade kind.

NOTE: The oil is hot enough for deep frying when small bubbles rise around a wooden spoon dipped in the oil.

KHORESHT-E QORMEH SABZI

LAMB IN A HERB SAUCE

SERVES 4

80g (2³/₄oz) red kidney beans

large bunch (sufficent to fill half a cup when chopped)
  each chives and flat-leaf parsley

large bunch fresh spinach (sufficent to fill a quarter of a cup
  when cooked)

500g (1lb 4oz) lamb (shoulder with bone)

oil

1 large onion

1 teaspoon turmeric

¹/₄ teaspoon saffron, ground

1¹/₂ tablespoons dried fenugreek

2 *limu omani* (dried limes)

1–2 tablespoons verjuice (available in small bottles
  from Persian shops and some supermarkets),
  or 2–3 tablespoons freshly squeezed lemon juice

1 teaspoon butter

salt, pepper

YOU WILL ALSO NEED:

4 servings of *chelo* (rice), *see* recipe page 72

1 The day before you plan to cook the dish, rinse the
beans and leave to soak overnight. The next day, drain in a
sieve and rinse with fresh water.

2 Meanwhile, wash the herbs and spinach and shake dry.
Remove all the stalks from the parsley, then finely chop
the leaves together with the chives and spinach.

3 Wash the rice for *chelo* in several changes of water, drain,
and soak for at least 25 minutes in a bowl of cold water to
which 1 tablespoon salt has been added.

4 Strip the meat from the bone and cut into small cubes,
then set aside.

5 Heat some oil in a large pan. Add the fresh chopped
herbs and the spinach and fry for 20 minutes over a low
to medium heat, without any additional liquid, stirring
occasionally, taking care not to let the herbs turn black.
Set aside.

6 Finely chop the onion. Heat some oil in a large pan and
fry the onion until golden. Sprinkle the turmeric over the
onion and stir once.

7 Add the cubes of lamb and fry for 8–10 minutes until
the meat is lightly browned on all sides.

8 Add the bone to the pan, sprinkle with pepper and
saffron, and stir. Add the dried fenugreek and stir everything once more.

9 Prick the limes all over with a fork. Add to the pan
along with the kidney beans and pour in 500ml (18fl oz)
hot water. Stir everything, then cover and boil for 10
minutes. Reduce the heat and simmer gently for 1 hour.

10 When the meat and beans have been cooking for
about 1 hour, drain the soaked rice in a sieve and put on
to cook (follow the recipe on page 72).

11 As soon as the rice is steaming (second stage of
cooking), add the sautéed herbs, *verjuice* (or lemon juice)
and butter to the meat in the pan, and season generously
with salt.

12 Meanwhile, stir the sauce, replace the lid and continue
to simmer gently for at least 1 hour. If the level of liquid
in the pan gets too low, top up with a little cold water as
necessary; this makes the oil rise to the surface, allowing
the flavours to penetrate better. In principle, however, the
less water that evaporates and needs to be replaced, the
better. Flavour escapes along with the steam, and the
khoresh is meant to be thick. If, on the other hand, the stew
becomes too much like soup, with the ingredients swim-
ming in the liquid, leave the lid open a little to allow the
excess liquid to evaporate.

13 Ladle the *khoresh* into an attractive bowl, spoon the
rice onto a platter and serve.

TIP: The herbs for the classic *khoresht-e qormeh sabzi* are
available dried and ready-mixed in Persian shops. For 4
servings, you'll need about 60–70g (2¹/₄–2¹/₂oz). The dried
herbs must also be soaked for 10 minutes, drained then
gently sautéed separately in a little oil in a small pan for
about 10 minutes before cooking. This is best done over a
low-to-medium heat, as the herbs must never be allowed
to turn black, or they will taste bitter.

KHORESHT-E KARAFS

LAMB WITH CELERY

SERVES 4

1 head celery

oil

200g (7oz) each fresh parsley and mint (if fresh mint is not
    available, substitute 1 heaped tablespoon dried mint)

500g (1lb 2oz) lamb (shoulder with bone)

1 large onion

1 teaspoon turmeric

1/2 teaspoon saffron, ground

salt, pepper

1–2 tablespoons *verjuice* (available in Persian shops and some
    supermarkets), or 2 tablespoons freshly squeezed lemon
    juice

1 teaspoon butter

YOU WILL ALSO NEED:

4 servings of rice, *see* recipe page 72

1   Trim the celery, removing the leaves and any tough
outer fibres. Slice the stalks into short (2cm/1-inch) pieces
and fry in a pan in a little oil over a medium heat until
golden. Set aside.

2   Wash and shake dry the fresh herbs; remove and discard
the stalks and finely chop the leaves.

3   Strip the meat from the bone and cut it into cubes.

4   Heat a little oil in a pan and sauté the fresh herbs for
about 20 minutes, stirring. Do not allow the herbs to
turn black.

5   Finely chop the onion. Heat some oil in a large pan
and fry until soft and golden. Sprinkle over the turmeric
and stir once.

6   Add the cubed lamb to the onions in the pan and fry
for 8–10 minutes, until the meat is lightly browned on
all sides. Add the bone to the pan to give the sauce some
additional flavour.

7   Sprinkle the saffron over the meat and season generously
with pepper. If using dried mint, add it to the meat at this
stage and stir once.

8   Add the sautéed herbs and the celery to the lamb with
500ml (18fl oz) water. Stir, cover, bring to the boil, then
reduce the heat and simmer over a low heat for 1 1/2 hours.

9   While the meat is braising, wash the rice in several
changes of water, drain, and soak for 25 minutes in a bowl
of cold water to which 1 tablespoon salt has been added.
Drain well, then set the rice on to cook, steaming it for
60–70 minutes (*see* recipe on page 72).

10   When the meat has been cooking for 1 hour, season
with salt, and stir in the *verjuice* (or lemon juice) and the
butter. If the level of liquid in the pan gets too low, top
up with cold water as necessary. The cold water causes the
oil to rise to the surface, helping the flavours to penetrate
more. However, in principle the less water that evaporates
and needs be replaced, the better. Flavour escapes along
with the steam, and the *khoresh* is actually meant to be
quite thick. On the other hand, if there is too much liquid
in the pan and the dish resembles a soup with the ingredients floating in it, leave the lid slightly open until the
excess liquid has evaporated.

11   Serve the *khoresh* as soon as the steamed rice is cooked.

Right and opposite: Goats glean
sufficient nourishment from even
the most arid strips of land.

KHORESHT-E FESENJAN
DUCK WITH WALNUTS AND POMEGRANATE

SERVES 4

FOR THE WALNUT SAUCE:

400g (14oz) walnut kernels

1 medium onion

oil

1/2 teaspoon turmeric

4–5 tablespoons pomegranate syrup (available in Persian shops and some supermarkets)

salt

FOR THE DUCK:

2 large duck legs and 1 breast (see also Variation)

1 large onion

1/2 teaspoon turmeric

salt, pepper

1/2 teaspoon saffron, ground

2–3 bay leaves

oil

YOU WILL ALSO NEED:

4 servings of *chelo* (rice), *see* recipe page 72

1 Grind the walnuts very finely in a blender or grinder (*see* Tip).

2 Finely chop the onion. Heat a little oil in a large pan and fry until golden. Sprinkle with the turmeric and stir once.

3 Add the ground walnuts to the onions and fry for 3–4 minutes, until the walnuts are lightly toasted and their fragrance rises. (Take care not to allow them to turn too dark, however, or they will taste bitter.)

4 Pour in 500ml (18fl oz) water, cover, and simmer over a low heat, stirring occasionally (it will cook for 3 hours in total, *see* Note). To prevent the sauce from thickening too much, top up with 250ml (9fl oz) cold water from time to time. Cold water causes the oil from the nuts to rise gradually to the surface, helping the flavours to penetrate.

5 When the nut sauce has been cooking for an hour, prepare the duck. First rinse the duck pieces in cold water and pull off the skin (this is best done by holding the pieces firmly with a paper towel to get a grip). Halve the breast and cut the legs in two at the joint.

6 Peel and quarter the onion. Heat some oil in a large, deep pan and stir-fry the onion pieces for about 5 minutes, until golden. Sprinkle with the turmeric, and season with salt and pepper.

7 Place the meat on top of the onions and sprinkle with the ground saffron. Add the bay leaves and cover with a lid. Let everything sear for 5 minutes.

8 Now pour in about 80ml (2³/₄oz) boiling water, reduce the heat to low, cover, and braise the duck for a good hour. You should be left with a little concentrated liquid at the end of the cooking time; if necessary, top up with a drop of water or leave the lid open slightly to allow any excess liquid to evaporate.

9 As soon as the duck is braising in the pan, add the pomegranate syrup to the simmering nuts, stir, and let the sauce continue to cook over a low heat for another hour.

10 While everything is cooking, wash the rice in several changes of water, drain, and soak for an hour in cold water to which 1 tablespoon salt has been added.

11 Next, add the braised duck together with the onions and pan juices to the nut sauce, and season with salt. Now cover the pan, and braise the duck in the nut sauce over a very low heat for an additional hour.

12 As soon as the duck is braising in the nut sauce, put the rice on to cook in a large non-stick pan and steam for about 60–70 minutes, so that the rice and meat will be ready at the same time.

TIP: The walnuts can also be pounded in a large mortar, or chopped very finely on a board with a broad-bladed knife – although both options are hard work.

NOTE: *Khoresht-e fesenjan* is a unique dish – for many, the crowning glory of all *khoresh*. A dish prepared for special occasions, its luxurious nature is famous. In Iran, an arrogant person might be described as 'behaving as if he'd had partridge and *fesenjan*'! Traditionally, the walnuts are actually simmered for up to 5 hours over a very low heat – 3 hours is the bare minimum. If you have the time, therefore, make an early start, as the longer and more gently the nuts simmer, the more aromatic the finished sauce will turn out. The preparation of *khoresht-e fesenjan* may sound rather complex and time-consuming – but the end result is really worthwhile.

VARIATION: Chicken is often used as a substitute for duck in this dish, and makes a popular alternative. Either cut up a whole chicken into 8 portions, or use 4 large, skinned chicken legs, halved at the joint.

KHORESHT-E ALU
CHICKEN WITH PRUNES

SERVES 4

2 large onions

4 large chicken legs

oil, salt, pepper

1 teaspoon turmeric

400g (14oz) *alu* (yellow prunes, available in
  Persian shops)

50g (1³/₄oz) sultanas (optional)

¹/₂ teaspoon saffron, ground

YOU WILL ALSO NEED:

4 servings of rice, *see* recipe page 72 or 73

1 Peel the onions and slice thinly.

2 Wash the chicken legs and cut in two at the joint. In a
large pan, heat some oil and sear the chicken pieces all over
until the skin is golden. Lift the chicken pieces out and set
aside on a plate.

3 Place the pan back on the heat, add a little more oil,
and place over a moderate heat. Add the sliced onion and
stir-fry for about 3 minutes, until browned.

4 Sprinkle the turmeric over the onions, add the *alu* and
fry for about 5 minutes. Add the sultanas and saffron and
de-glaze with 125ml (4fl oz) boiling water.

5 Add the chicken pieces, season with salt and pepper,
cover, and braise for about 5 minutes at a moderate heat.

6 Pour in a further 125ml (4fl oz) of boiling water,
reduce the heat to low, cover, and simmer the *khoresh* for a
good 1¹/₂ hours (there should be a scant 250ml (8–9fl oz)
of liquid left in the pan at the end of cooking).

7 As soon as the *khoresh* is braising in the pan, prepare the
rice so that both will be ready at the same time.

KHORESHT-E ALU QORMEH GHEISI
LAMB WITH APRICOTS

SERVES 4

60g (2¹/₄oz) *lapeh* (yellow lentils)

2 large onions

oil, salt, pepper

1 teaspoon turmeric

500g (1lb 2oz) lamb (boneless shoulder), cut into
  medium-sized cubes

150g (5¹/₂oz) *alu* (yellow prunes, available
  in Persian shops)

200g (7oz) dried apricots, halved

2 tablespoons dried fenugreek leaves

¹/₂ teaspoon saffron, ground

1 generous pinch ground nutmeg

YOU WILL ALSO NEED:

4 servings of rice, *see* recipe page 72

Left: Many inhabitants of the little town of Abyaneh remained
faithful to the teachings of Zoroaster, even after Islamization.

1 The day before you plan to cook the dish, pour boiling
water over the *lapeh* and leave to soak overnight. The next
day, drain in a sieve and rinse with fresh water.

2 Finely chop the onions and fry in a large pan in a little
oil until golden. Sprinkle over the turmeric and stir.

3 Add the pieces of lamb and fry for 5 minutes until
browned on all sides.

4 Now add the drained *lapeh*, dried fruits and fenugreek
leaves to the lamb and stir-fry for 5 minutes.

5 Sprinkle with the saffron and nutmeg, season with salt
and pepper, and stir once.

6 Pour over 250ml (9fl oz) boiling water and bring the
khoresh to the boil. Reduce the heat to low, cover, and
simmer gently for at least 2 hours. If the level of liquid
in the pan falls too low, top it up with boiling water as
needed. Don't overdo it though, as the *khoresh* is meant
to be thick.

7 As soon as the *khoresh* is braising in the pan, prepare
the rice so that both will be ready at the same time.

8 Serve with yogurt.

ABGUSHT-E SADEH
LAMB STEW WITH QUINCE

SERVES 4–6

60g (2¼oz) each dried chickpeas, haricot beans
  and red kidney beans
3 *limu omani* (dried limes)
1 large onion
1kg (2¼lb) lamb (neck or leg, with bone)
2 teaspoons turmeric
½ teaspoon cinnamon
1 potato
½ quince (or 1 small apple)
salt, pepper

YOU WILL ALSO NEED:
fresh flatbread, for serving

1 The day before you plan to cook the dish, rinse the
pulses and leave them to soak overnight. The next day,
drain in a sieve and rinse with fresh water.
2 Prick the dried limes in several places with a fork.
Halve the onion and place it in a large pan along with the
lamb, pulses, limes, turmeric and cinnamon. Season with
pepper and pour over 2 litres (70fl oz) water.
3 Bring all the ingredients to the boil over a high heat,
boil for 10 minutes, then reduce the heat to low, cover, and
simmer for at least 2 hours.
4 Now add the potato, quince (or apple) and season with
salt. Simmer for a good 2 hours more. There should be
about 1 litre (35fl oz) of liquid left in the pan at the end
of the cooking time.
5 Pour the contents of the pan into a sieve set over a
small pan. Keep the resulting broth warm over the lowest
heat setting.
6 Leave the solid ingredients remaining in the sieve to
cool slightly, then lift out the meat and limes. Strip the
meat from the bone and return the meat to the large pan.
Halve and de-seed the limes and return them to the pan
with the meat. The taste of lime is strong – if you prefer a
less dominant taste, put only 1 lime back into the pan.
7 Using a large pestle, pound all the ingredients in the
pan until you have a coarse purée.

8 Serve the pounded meat and the broth separately, with
flatbread either crumbled into the broth, or placed on the
plate with the broth poured on top.

TIP: A few garlic cloves, finely chopped and fried in a
little oil until golden, make a fine garnish and are a good
accompaniment for this dish. Serve *torshi* (sour pickled
vegetables), fresh radishes, and red onions on the side.

NOTE: In Iran, special crockery is used for *abgusht*, consisting of a small, lidded pan made of ceramic or metal,
a large plate with a slightly raised edge, and a pestle with
a slightly flattened base (*see* photograph page 97). At the
table, the solid ingredients are spooned out of the little
pan and pounded with the pestle on the plate.

Right: In the background of this photograph
the outline of an ancient *caravanserai* can be seen.

ABGUSHT-E BOZBASH

LAMB AND HERB STEW

SERVES 4–6

60g (2¹/₄oz) each dried chickpeas, haricot beans
    and red kidney beans

3 *limu omani* (dried limes)

1 large onion

oil

large bunch (sufficient to fill half a cup when chopped)
    each fresh flat-leaf parsley, chives and coriander, chopped

2 tablespoons dried fenugreek leaves

1kg (2¹/₄lb) lamb with bone (neck or leg)

2 teaspoons turmeric

2 potatoes

salt, pepper

YOU WILL ALSO NEED:

fresh flatbread for serving

1 The day before you plan to cook the dish, rinse the pulses and leave them to soak overnight. The next day, drain in a sieve and rinse in fresh water.

2 Prick the dried limes in several places with a fork.

3 Halve the onion. Finely chop one of the halves and fry in a large pan in a little oil until golden.

4 Add the chopped fresh herbs and fry for 7–8 minutes, stirring occasionally. Now add the dried fenugreek leaves, stir once, and set aside.

5 Place the lamb, the remaining half onion, pulses, limes and turmeric in a large pan and season with pepper. Pour in 2 litres (70fl oz) water. Bring to the boil and boil vigorously for 10 minutes over a high heat, then reduce the heat, cover and simmer gently for 2 hours.

6 Add the potatoes and the herb and onion mixture, and salt. Simmer for a further 2 hours. There should be 1 litre (35fl oz) of liquid left at the end of the cooking time.

7 Pour the stew into a sieve set over a small pan, and keep the resulting broth warm over the lowest possible heat.

8 Lift out the limes and lamb and strip the meat from the bone. Halve and de-seed the limes. Return all the solid ingredients (minus the bone) to the large pan, and pound them with a pestle to a coarse purée.

9 Serve the pounded meat and the broth separately, with flatbread as an accompaniment.

ABGUSHT-E KASHK

CHICKPEA STEW

SERVES 4

160g (5³/₄oz) dried chickpeas

6 tablespoons *kashk* (or sour cream)

oil

2 teaspoons dried mint

1 large onion

1kg (2¹/₄ lb) lamb with bone (neck or leg)

2 teaspoons turmeric

salt, pepper

YOU WILL ALSO NEED:

fresh flatbread, for serving

1 The day before you plan to cook the dish, rinse the chickpeas and soak overnight in a generous amount of water. The next day, drain in a sieve and rinse in fresh water.

2 Boil the *kashk* uncovered in a small saucepan with 250ml (9fl oz) water for 20 minutes, stirring occasionally to prevent sticking.

3 Heat some oil in a small pan. Rub the mint to a fine powder between your fingers and sprinkle into the hot oil, stirring once. As soon as the fragrance of the mint begins to rise, remove from the heat and tip into a small bowl. Set aside.

4 Peel and halve the onion and place in a large pan along with the lamb and chickpeas. Sprinkle over turmeric and season with pepper. Add 2 litres (70fl oz) water and bring everything to the boil. Turn the heat to low, cover, and simmer for about 2 hours.

5 Now season with salt, cover, and simmer for a further hour, until only about 1 litre (35fl oz) of liquid remains in the pan.

6 Pour the stew through a sieve set over a small pan. Add about two-thirds of the *kashk* to the resulting broth and bring it back to the boil (if you are using sour cream, make sure that it does not boil from this point on). Keep the broth warm by gently heating over the lowest heat setting.

7 Leave the solid ingredients remaining in the sieve to cool slightly, then lift out the meat and strip it from the bone, discarding the bone. Return the meat to the big pan along with the rest of the solid ingredients in the sieve.

8 Add the remaining *kashk* or sour cream to the meat and chickpea mixture in the pan, and pound everything until you obtain a coarse purée.

9 Serve the pounded meat and the broth separately, with flatbread either crumbled into the broth or placed on the plate with the broth poured on top.

TIP: To serve *abgusht* in the traditional way, hand round the broth in attractive soup bowls with a little sautéed mint and some flatbread. The bread can be eaten either in slices or crumbled into the soup. Serve the pounded meat and vegetable mixture on flat plates to the side, sprinkled with the rest of the mint. *Abgusht* is always accompanied by *torshi* (sour pickled vegetables), fresh radishes and onions.

Above: Old, colourful saddlebags are still in use today, even if the forms of transport they are used with are unorthodox.

Following pages: Abgusht is rarely served in restaurants, so people seize the chance to sample it when it appears on the menu.

DRAKHT-I ASURIG
THE PARTHIAN FABLE OF THE DATE-PALM AND THE GOAT

From ancient Mesopotamia a wealth of fables has survived, in which rivals such as bird and fish, cow and horse, tree and grass fight over which of the two is more important for mankind. Such fables were also popular in ancient Persia. The poem *Drakht-i asurig* ('The Assyrian Tree'), in which a date-palm and a goat argue over their relative importance to man, was probably written on Persian soil before the birth of Christ. Originally versified in the Parthian language, the verbal duel also acquired a number of Middle Persian elements during the course of being handed down. First, the palm begins to list its advantages:

> Kings eat of my fruit.
> I am planks and the masts of ships.
> Brooms are made of me to sweep home and hearth,
> And pestles to grind rice and barley,
> And fans for the fire.
> I am vinegar for peasants, honey for the Nobility.
> I am a nest for small birds, shade for wayfarers,
> My head will be green for eternity,
> And he who is lacking bread[1] and wine[2] can make free with me.

[1]Bread: stoned, thinly sliced, sun-dried and pounded dates were boiled in salted water; wheat- or barley-flour was added, and the whole was kneaded into a bread dough.
[2]Wine: there is a long tradition of date-wine in Persia.

But then the goat retorted:

> Without me, no one can venerate
> The all-powerful, radiant Creator *Ahura Mazda*[3]
> For I provide the milk (for the *hom*[4] ritual).
> No one makes saddlebags without me, for I am the goat;
> Belts, embroidered with pearls, shoes for the Nobility, finger-stalls for the courtiers.
> Water hoses they make from my pelt, for desert and steppe.
> Parchment they fashion from my skin,
> And bills and contracts are written on me.
> Fine coats they weave from my goat hair.
> I am milk and *dugh*, yoghurt and *kashk*.
> He who goes to market with less than ten silver drachmas
> Need not bother to approach the goat.
> Dates are bought by children for two copper pieces.
> This is my golden speech, which I have aimed at you,
> As one who casts pearls before swine[5],
> Or plays the harp before a drunken camel.

[3]*Ahura Mazda* (Middle Persian *Ohrmazd*, Modern Persian *Hormuz*): the high god of the Zoroastrian religion.
[4]Milk and *hom*: the ritual intoxicating beverage *hom* (Sanskrit *soma*) was mixed with milk for greater digestibility.
[5]Pearls before swine: the familiar Biblical quotation from Matthew 7:6 probably stems from Persian tradition. It is further illustrated here in the line about the lowbrow camel.

From the Persian point of view, the goat obviously holds more trump cards. Previously, in ancient Mesopotamia, the date-palm had always won such arguments. The Persians, though – however much they appreciated and venerated the date-palm – clearly recalled their nomadic origins in which sheep and goats formed the basis of the food supply

Translated according to M. Navvābi, 'Manzume-ye Deraxt-i azurig', Tehran, 1346.

KHORAK-E LUBIA SABZ

BRAISED MEAT WITH GREEN BEANS

SERVES 4

500g (1lb 2oz) boneless veal or lamb

250g (9oz) fresh green beans

1 onion

olive oil, salt, pepper

1/2 teaspoon hot red paprika

1 teaspoon turmeric

200g (1 medium can) canned tomatoes

2 medium potatoes, peeled

YOU WILL ALSO NEED:

fresh flatbread for serving

1 Cut the meat into small cubes. Wash and trim the beans, then halve them.

2 Peel and finely chop the onion. Heat some oil in a large pan and fry the onion until golden.

3 Add the meat to the onions, sprinkle with the paprika and turmeric, and fry for about 5 minutes, stirring.

4 Add the tomatoes with the juice from the can. Cover, and simmer over a low heat for about 1 hour, until the sauce has thickened. Top up with a little hot water as needed; do not use cold water, which would make the meat tough. Remember, though, that this dish is meant to be thick, with the consistency of a stew, not a soup.

5 Add the green beans along with 6 tablespoons hot water. Season with pepper and simmer gently for a further 30 minutes.

6 Finely dice the potatoes, add them to the pan, and season with salt. Simmer the *khorak* for a further hour.

KHORAK-E MAHICHEH

LEG OF LAMB

SERVES 4

1kg (2¹/ lb) leg of lamb (with bone)

1 large onion, quartered

4 garlic cloves

1 teaspoon turmeric

2 bay leaves

1 tablespoon pepper

2 tomatoes (optional)

salt

YOU WILL ALSO NEED:

boiled potatoes or fresh flatbread, for serving

1 Put the meat into a pan with just enough water to cover; bring to the boil, skimming off any scum that forms.

2 Add the quartered onion, whole peeled garlic cloves, turmeric, pepper and bay leaves. Cover the pan and simmer for 2 hours, topping up with boiling water whenever the water level recedes below the top of the meat.

3 About halfway through the cooking time, scald and skin the tomatoes. Add them to the meat, season generously with salt, cover, and continue to simmer.

4 The dish is done once the liquid has thickened and the meat comes away easily from the bone. There should be about 500ml (18fl oz) of liquid left in the pan at the end of the cooking time.

TIP: Remember that the lid should be lifted off the pan as little as possible while the dish is cooking.

NOTE: *Khorak* is a type of goulash consisting mainly of meat, and served with bread or potatoes. The taste of the *khorak* depends to a great extent on the quality of the meat and the length of the cooking time – if possible, let the stew simmer gently for up to 4 hours. If time is short, make the stew in a pressure cooker (check exact cooking times). In this dish, the flavour of the meat is really brought out, and it pays to use best-quality meat.

Right: One of the highlights of any trip to Iran, the Emam Mosque in Isfahan is one of the most beautiful in the world.

KHORAK-E KUFTEH GHELGHELI

LITTLE MEATBALLS

SERVES 4

2 onions (1 small, 1 medium-sized)
500g (1lb 2oz) minced (ground) lamb
250g (9oz) carrots
oil
1 teaspoon turmeric
2 medium potatoes
1 tablespoon tomato paste
salt, pepper

1 Grate the small onion, mix with the minced (ground) lamb and season with salt and pepper. Roll the mixture into small meatballs and set aside on waxed paper.
2 Peel the carrots and slice into thin rounds and set aside.
3 Finely chop the medium-sized onion. Heat a little oil in a large pan and fry the onion until golden. Sprinkle over the turmeric and stir once.

4 Pour in 150ml (5fl oz) boiling water. As soon as the pan comes to the boil, reduce the heat and carefully slide the meatballs and carrots into the pan. Cover, and simmer very gently over a low heat for 1 hour, taking care not to let the meatballs break apart.
5 Peel and finely dice the potatoes.
6 Add the tomato paste to the pan and stir carefully to mix. Stir in the diced potatoes and season to taste with salt and pepper.
7 Let everything simmer with the lid on for a further hour or so, until the sauce has thickened. Top up with a little boiling water as needed.

TIP: This is a typical early autumn dish that my mother cooks. She serves it accompanied with flatbread, yogurt, fresh herbs, spring onions, radishes, and some seedless green grapes.

KHORAK-E ZABAN

TONGUE WITH MUSHROOMS

SERVES 4

1 calf's tongue
1 small bunch parsley
1 large onion, quartered
4 garlic cloves
1–2 bay leaves
1 teaspoon turmeric
500g (1lb 2oz) mushrooms
3 tablespoons butter
1 tablespoon flour
salt, pepper

1 Wash the tongue and remove the skin with a small, sharp knife. Wash the parsley and finely chop the leaves of 3–4 stalks. Tie together the remaining parsley stalks with some kitchen twine.
2 Place the tongue in a large pan and add enough water to cover completely (about 2 litres/70fl oz). Add the onion along with the garlic cloves, parsley stalks and bay leaves. Sprinkle with turmeric and season with salt and pepper.

3 Bring everything to the boil, skimming off the scum as it forms. Cover the pan and simmer for 2 hours. At the end of the cooking time there should be slightly more than 500ml (18fl oz) of liquid left in the pan.
4 Wipe and trim the mushrooms and slice them thinly. Heat 1 tablespoon butter in a pan and fry the mushrooms over a medium heat until slightly browned.
5 Heat the remaining butter in a small saucepan. Add the flour and sweat, stirring continuously, until golden. Pour in 1 cupful of the stock from the tongue and bring the sauce to the boil, stirring all the time. Remove the sauce from the heat and add the mushrooms. If the sauce is too thick, add more stock.
6 To serve, carve the tongue crossways into thin slices, and arrange on an oval platter with some mushroom sauce and a little chopped parsley sprinkled on top.

TIP: The tongue can also be cooked in a pressure cooker (check exact cooking times). The skin is a great deal easier to remove from the tongue after it is cooked.

GRILLED AND PAN-FRIED MEAT DISHES

KEBAB AND *KUFTEH*

Kebab is one of Iran's most typical dishes, and has little in common with the rotating spits of the street vendors of Turkey.

The residents of Tehran enjoy going to a *kebab khane,* or grill house, especially on days off. The meat (*kebab* in Persian) is threaded onto thin, flat metal skewers. These restaurants compete to see who can serve the tenderest meat on the longest skewer, with one famous Tehran grill house offering its diners a special skewer no less than half a metre long!

The tastiness and tenderness of the meat are primarily determined by its quality, and this motto applies equally to all Persian cuisine: never skimp on the ingredients. Persian cooking is not a 'cuisine for cheats' and is as good as its raw materials. The delicacy of the recipes and the choice of seasonings is geared towards this. Seasonings devised to rescue insipid meat are unknown in Persian cooking, which relies on high-quality, appetizing meat whose inherent flavour has no need of a boost.

Even so, good meat can still be enhanced by marinating it before cooking. Leaving the meat in the marinade for a few hours, or even overnight, allows the flavours to penetrate fully. For *jujeh kebab* the chicken will often be skinned and boned beforehand, allowing the marinade to permeate the meat more effectively. Sometimes, however, the chicken legs are left intact and are marinated with the skin still on, then placed directly onto the grill without skewering.

In Iran, the marinated, boned pieces of meat are always threaded onto the typical long, flattened skewers and placed on a charcoal grill, giving the Persian *kebab* its unique and unmistakeable flavour. However, the underlying truth is that it is scarcely possible to prepare a *kebab* like this at home unless you have access to an open fire. Skewered *kebab* is ideal for an afternoon barbecue on the shores of a lake, or an evening barbecue party. In the home kitchen, people cook more modest *kebab* or opt for pan-braised *kufteh.*

JUJEH KABAB
MARINATED CHICKEN

SERVES 4
1 chicken or 4 chicken legs
butter for basting

INGREDIENTS FOR THE MARINADES
(ALL FOR 1kg/2¼lb MEAT):

FOR A LEMON MARINADE (CLASSIC):
juice of 2 lemons (or 8–9 limes)
1 onion, finely grated
1 tablespoon oil (optional)
½ teaspoon saffron, ground
2 teaspoons freshly ground black pepper
salt

FOR A YOGURT MARINADE:
250ml (9fl oz) yogurt (as sour a variety as possible)
1 tablespoon finely grated onion
½ teaspoon saffron, ground
2 teaspoons freshly ground black pepper
salt

FOR A SOY SAUCE MARINADE:
125ml (4fl oz) groundnut oil
4 tablespoons dark soy sauce
1 teaspoon finely chopped fresh ginger
½ teaspoon honey
2 garlic cloves (optional)

YOU WILL ALSO NEED:
4 servings of rice (chelo) (see recipe, page 72).
Begin preparations for the chelo about 1½ hours before you plan to serve the meal.
Flat-bladed metal kebab skewers, 30–50cm (12–20-inches) long (available from Persian shops or kitchenware stores)

1 If using a whole chicken, wash and cut it into six or eight pieces. You can opt to de-bone it if you like, and use the bones to make stock. If you are only using chicken legs, halve them at the joint, then skin them and remove the bones (see Note).
2 In a large bowl, mix together the ingredients for your choice of marinade. Add the chicken pieces to the marinade, turning them so that they are all coated. Cover the bowl and refrigerate for at least 3 hours, or ideally overnight.

3 Just before grilling the chicken pieces, thread them onto the metal skewers. Thread each breast piece onto its own skewer; as they are leaner than the leg pieces they will need to be watched closely to ensure they do not become too dry.
4 Baste the meat frequently as it grills, alternating the marinade with a little melted butter. Grill it over a moderate heat, skin-side-down, for 8–10 minutes, then turn it over and grill the other side for a further 8–10 minutes, or until cooked through. The best way to tell if it is cooked is to remove a piece and cut it in half; the juices should run clear and there should be no sign of blood.

TIP: If you intend to pan-braise the chicken, the yogurt marinade is the best choice. Coarsely chop an onion, then fry it in a large pan in a little oil or butter until it becomes translucent. Thread the marinated cubes of chicken onto small wooden skewers, place them in the pan, and dot with a little butter. Cover the pan and braise gently for an hour. This method is easy and highly digestible.

NOTE: Strictly speaking, *Jujeh kebab* is traditionally made with poussins (young chickens), but ordinary chicken is often used instead. The younger the chicken, of course, the more tender and delicate-tasting the *kebab* will be.

Chicken legs can also be placed right onto the grill without skewering. De-boning the delicate legs requires a certain amount of skill and patience, as well as a really sharp knife, but once stripped from the bones, the meat is very easy to thread onto the skewers. An alternative would be to buy ready-boned chicken breasts. Cut these into large cubes, then marinate them and thread them onto the skewers.

Whether or not you skin the chicken before marinating is purely a question of personal taste: on the one hand, the marinade penetrates much better without skin, but on the other, the skin keeps the meat nice and juicy as it grills, and many people find that the crispy skin itself is a special treat.

Right: Even in the West there are numerous Persian restaurants where you can eat in the traditional style.

KEBAB-E KUBIDEH

SKEWERED MINCED MEAT

SERVES 4

3–4 onions

1kg (2¼lb) lamb and beef (500g/1lb 2oz each), finely
  ground and mixed together

1 teaspoon saffron, ground

2 teaspoons sumac (available from Persian or
  Turkish shops)

salt, pepper

8 small tomatoes

YOU WILL ALSO NEED:

Flat-bladed metal *kebab* skewers 30–50 cm (12–16-inches) long
(available in Persian shops and good kitchenware stores)

1 Finely grate the onions and, using your fingers, squeeze
or press them gently against a sieve to remove the juice.

2 Mix the grated onion pulp well with the ground meat.

3 Dissolve the saffron in about 20ml (¾fl oz) of hot
water and add to the meat. Sprinkle with the sumac,
season with salt and pepper, and mix everything well.

4 Place the ground meat mixture in a large pan and, with
your hands, knead it for 10 minutes over the lowest heat.

5 Now put the meat onto the skewers – this may take
a bit of practice. The best way is to shape the mixture on a
chopping board into a firm sausage. This should measure
about three fingers wide and two fingers thick, and be
quite a lot shorter than the skewer. Now carefully push
the skewer lengthways through the meat, reshaping the
sausage as necessary. Thread a tomato on each end and grill
the skewers over a medium barbecue until cooked
through, turning frequently.

TIP: *Kebab-e kubideh* is served with flatbread, fresh flat-leaf
parsley (basil is also sometimes used) and fresh onions.
Place a small bowl of sumac on the table so that everyone
can season their meat as they choose.

KEBAB-E BARG

FILLET KEBAB

SERVES 4

1kg (2¼lb) lamb fillet (hung if possible)

butter for basting

FOR THE MARINADE:

2 onions

4 tablespoons olive oil

salt, pepper

YOU WILL ALSO NEED:

flat-bladed metal *kebab* skewers 30–50cm (12–20-inches) long
(available in Persian shops and good kitchenware stores)

1 On the day before you want to serve the dish, cut the
lamb fillet into pieces about 5cm (2-inches) square and
1cm (½-inch) thick.

2 Finely grate the onions and, using your fingers, squeeze
well, ideally against a sieve. Discard the onion juices, mix
the pulp with the oil and season with salt and pepper.

3 Pound the pieces of lamb with a meat mallet or
heavy-handled knife to produce very thin, delicate 'leaves'
of meat. Mix the meat with the marinade, cover, and marinate overnight in the refrigerator.

4 The next day, thread the meat on to the skewers. Pound
the meat again, quite gently – this time using the blade of
the knife – so that the meat is covered in small incisions.

5 Grill the skewers over a moderately hot charcoal
barbecue, basting the meat frequently with melted butter
to stop it drying out, until cooked through.

TIP: *Kabab-e barg* is served with rice (*chelo*) or bread, and
with raw onions on the side. You could also put a small
bowl of sumac on the table, so that diners can season their
own meat if desired.

Right: In some areas of the Zagros Mountains,
nomads still use stone dwellings even today.

KEBAB TABEI

PAN-BRAISED MINCED MEAT

SERVES 4

1 large onion

600g (1lb 5oz) very finely minced (ground) beef or lamb

1 teaspoon turmeric

1 teaspoon curry powder

1 teaspoon hot red paprika

1/2 teaspoon sumac

salt, pepper

oil

200g (1 small can) canned tomatoes

4 garlic cloves, peeled and thinly sliced

1 Finely grate the onion and, using your fingers, squeeze or press the pulp gently against the sides of a sieve to remove the juice.

2 Mix the ground meat well with the onion pulp, turmeric, curry powder, paprika and sumac. Season with salt and pepper. Knead thoroughly until the ingredients are well-mixed. Moisten your hands and shape the mixture into a large, firm ball.

3 Pour a little oil into a large, deep pan. Press the meat mixture firmly down in the pan, until it covers the bottom completely, like a large pancake. Raise it slightly around the edge, making sure that it is firmly pressed down here too, as it will shrink as it cooks, and make sure there are no cracks in the meat.

4 Bring the pan up to a moderate heat. As soon as the meat is firm underneath – after about 10 minutes – cut the meat pancake lengthways into strips about 5cm (2-inches) wide, using a fish slice. Then turn the heat up briefly to a high setting, allowing the strips of meat to brown for 2 minutes.

5 Pour over the tomato juice from the can and place the tomatoes over the meat strips. If necessary, add a little water so that the meat is just covered. Sprinkle the sliced garlic over the top and season the sauce generously with salt and pepper. Reduce the heat to low, cover, and braise gently for 30 minutes without stirring, until cooked through.

TIP: Rice (*kateh* or *chelo*) or flatbread go well with this dish. Serve with yogurt and fresh onion rings, placing sumac, paprika and curry powder on the table so that people can season their own meat.

KOTLET-E DAST-E DAR

HANDMADE MEAT RISSOLES (PATTIES)

SERVES 4

2 large potatoes, peeled

1 carrot

1 medium onion, peeled

500g (1lb 2oz) minced (ground) beef

1 egg

1 teaspoon turmeric

salt, pepper, groundnut oil

1/2 teaspoon cinnamon

200g (7oz) breadcrumbs

1 Cook the potatoes in boiling water until just tender. Cook the carrot in boiling water until soft. Grate the potatoes, carrot and onion into a bowl.

2 In a large bowl, mix together the ground meat, egg and grated vegetables. Season with turmeric, salt, pepper, and cinnamon, and knead until thoroughly mixed.

3 Spread the breadcrumbs on a plate. Pinch off egg-sized pieces of the meat mixture and shape into balls. Flatten the balls between your palms, shaping them into flattish rissoles or patties. Coat the patties in the breadcrumbs and set aside on waxed paper.

4 Heat about 1cm (1/2-inch) oil in a non-stick pan. Once it is hot, brown the rissoles over a moderate heat on both sides, only turning when the underside is nice and brown.

TIP: Serve the rissoles warm or cold with flatbread, yogurt, spring onions (scallions), and radishes.

KUFTEH NOKHODCHI
MEAT DUMPLINGS

SERVES 4–6

500g (1lb 2oz) minced (ground) beef

1/2 teaspoon saffron, ground

1 teaspoon pepper

salt

300g (10 1/2oz) chickpea flour

2 onions

1/2 teaspoon turmeric

3–4 tablespoons vinegar

3 tablespoons sugar

oil

1 Mix the minced beef with the saffron and pepper, and season with salt. Knead until thoroughly mixed. Gradually add the chickpea flour, continuing to knead vigorously.

2 With moistened hands, shape the meat mixture into egg-sized balls and set aside on a piece of waxed paper.

3 Peel and finely chop the onions. Heat some oil in a large pan and fry the onions until soft and golden. Sprinkle with the turmeric and stir. Pour in 1 litre (35fl oz) hot water and bring to the boil, then lower the heat to a simmer.

4 Carefully slide the meat dumplings into the boiling water, cover, and simmer gently for around 1 1/2 hours over a low-to-moderate heat.

5 About 15 minutes before the end of the cooking time, combine the vinegar with the sugar and add to the pan. Continue simmering, leaving the lid open if necessary, so that you are left with a good 250ml (9fl oz) of sauce when the dumplings are done.

KUFTEH BERENJI
MEATBALLS WITH RICE

SERVES 4

80g (3oz) rice

salt, pepper

large bunch (sufficient to fill quarter of a cup when chopped) flat-leaf parsley

oil

250g (9oz) minced (ground) beef

1 egg

3 medium potatoes

1 green pepper

3 tomatoes

1 large onion

1 1/2 teaspoons turmeric

2 tablespoons tomato paste

2–3 tablespoons lemon juice

1 generous pinch saffron, ground

1 pinch sugar

1 Wash the rice and boil in 1 litre (35fl oz) of water, with a little salt, for 8–10 minutes, until *al dente,* then drain in a sieve. De-stalk the parsley and chop the leaves very finely.

2 Season the minced beef with salt and pepper and mix with the egg, cooked rice and parsley leaves, kneading well to combine thoroughly.

3 With moistened hands, shape the meat mixture into egg-sized balls. In a large pan, brown the meatballs in plenty of oil over a moderate heat, then drain on paper towels.

4 Peel the potatoes and wash the green pepper and the tomatoes. Chop the vegetables into small chunks. Peel and quarter the onion.

5 Heat some oil in a large pan and sauté the onion until golden. Sprinkle with turmeric and stir once. Spread the other vegetables over the sautéed onions, top with the meatballs and lower the heat.

6 Combine the tomato paste with the lemon juice, saffron, sugar, salt and pepper in a bowl with 250ml (9fl oz) boiling water and pour over the meatballs. Cover the pan and braise the meatballs over a low heat for 1 1/2 hours.

Right: It is useful to have the services of a porter or *barbar* to negotiate the long passages in the bazaar.

REGIONAL SPECIALTIES AND SAFAVID CUISINE

Few countries harbour such stark contrasts as Iran – in landscape and climate, population and history. The climate in the north, in Gilan and Mazandaran on the Caspian Sea, is temperate-Mediterranean; the southern provinces of Bushehr and Hormozgan on the Persian Gulf are tropically hot, very humid, and are among the most perspiration-inducing places on Earth. The great central basins are uninhabitable deserts. Their eastern border areas towards Afghanistan and Pakistan – southern Khorasan, Sistan and Baluchestan – have little water, and the strong 120-day summer wind blows away the topsoil.

The western and northern border areas – Kerman, Yazd, Isfahan and Tehran – have a better climate, but the air is very dry here also, and the climate is Continental, with stark contrasts of temperature. Still, the west and the northwest have water. The water for Isfahan comes from the Zagros Mountains, while the water for Tehran comes from the Alborz (Elburz) range. Both of these mountain ranges constitute worlds of their own – the Alborz massif with its Damavand peak stand more than 5,000 metres (16,500 feet) high, the focus of many myths, and the towering Zagros Mountains contain fertile plains and a wild, sometimes inaccessible semi-massifs.

Agriculture in the Zagros Mountains and in Azerbaijan is possible, in part thanks to the rainfall, and in part due to simple irrigation. In the arid border zones of the central deserts, irrigation has protected against evaporation of water from the land for thousands of years by the ingenious *qanat* system of underground channels.

Four cultivation zones are distinguishable in Iran: in the warmest and totally frost-free *Garmsir* zone, dates, sugar cane, and other tropical fruits flourish; the second, still warm zone, with only occasional frosts, is host to figs, pomegranates, peaches, almonds, rice, tobacco, sesame, grape vines and much else; the cooler and considerably higher-lying *Sardsir* zone offers the climate for all kinds of grains (except rice, which requires warmth), potatoes and fruit. Finally, in the harshest zone (*Sarhadd*), only sedentary or nomadic pasture management is possible.

The greatest conflict has traditionally arisen around the best climate zones. New conquerors would drive out long-established inhabitants. In times of stability, the image of what peoples belonged where has been reinforced. City-dwellers willingly believe that nomads prefer to live in barren territories, but even the nomads are not naturally equipped for the hard life in the least hospitable areas – only in times of great need can they, unlike farmers, seek refuge there and preserve their traditions and customs for generations.

Every bit as great as the differences between the population groups and their respective fates in Iran is the extent to which their cooking traditions have been adapted to regional conditions. The highlands of Azerbaijan allow extensive animal husbandry, and *kufteh Tabrizi* (Tabriz meatballs) are deservedly famous. Stockbreeding occurs throughout the whole of Iran, traditionally carried out by the nomads. As well as *kebab* dishes, many types of bread are also of nomadic origin. Not all breads are baked in large, walled ovens; one example is *nan-e sangak*, the stone bread that carries the imprint of the glowing-hot pebbles on which it was baked on the oven floor. A number of breads are also made in cast-iron pans, such as *nan-e saji*. The names of other types of bread still recall the peoples who introduced them, and who struck the native population as 'foreign': *nan-Barbari*, for example, the 'bread of the Barbars', named for a population group living south of Tehran during the Qajar era.

Especially significant for the history of Persian cuisine is the era of the *Safavids* (1501–1732). During this time, Persian cooking evolved into what it is today. The entire *polo* and *chelo* culture was stamped by the *Safavid* court chefs.

Despite great national unity, present-day Persian cooking also displays a few locally grown idiosyncracies. Rivers are found in the high mountains; thus *quezel ala* (trout) are a prized specialty there. Those living by lakes and the sea have a more lavish range to choose from. Typical of the Caspian Sea – in addition to caviar – is smoked fish, *mahi dudi*. Because of the climate, dishes from the south are generally less substantial than northern ones.

Right, and following pages: The reliefs in Persepolis not only demonstrate the skill of the stonemasons, but also provide a glimpse of the city's history.

QEZEL ALA
STUFFED TROUT

SERVES 4

4 small trout
4 tablespoons lemon juice
olive oil
salt
4–5 tablespoons sumac
25 walnut halves, coarsely chopped
4 garlic cloves, halved

1 Preheat the oven to 170°C/325°F/gas mark 3.
2 Gut and rinse the trout and brush them with lemon juice and some olive oil. Lay each trout in the centre of a large piece of aluminium foil. Season the fish evenly all over with salt and sumac, sprinkling as much of the sumac as possible inside the bellies of the trout.

3 Add the chopped walnuts and garlic, distributing them into the opened bellies.
4 Bring the sides of the foil together over each fish, folding to seal tightly. Bake in the preheated oven for about 45 minutes, then open out the foil and grill (broil) the trout for a further 7–10 minutes or so, until the skin is crisp and lightly browned.

TIP: Serve the trout with rice (*chelo* or *kateh*) or boiled potatoes.

VARIATION: Replace the sumac with ½ teaspoon saffron (finely ground in a mortar with a pinch of sugar, then dissolve in 3 tablespoons hot water), and place 1–2 sprigs of fresh flat-leaf parsley into the belly of each fish.

MAHI DUDI
SMOKED FISH FROM THE NORTH

SERVES 4

1 large smoked fish

YOU WILL ALSO NEED:
Sabzi polo (*see* recipe page 78)

1 Slice the fish open lengthways and remove the bones. Skin the fillets and cut them into large chunks (about 6cm/2½-inches).
2 Set the chunks of fish aside on a deep plate that will fit inside the rice pan.
3 Once the herb rice has been piled up in the pan at the beginning of the second stage of cooking, place the plate with the pieces of fish on top of the rice and cover with

the lid (without wrapping in the tea towel). This will allow the fish to be steamed and the drops of condensation that are formed to gradually collect on the plate with the fish.
4 After about 50 minutes steaming, wrap the lid in a tea towel (not earlier, as the condensation must first collect in the plate) and steam the rice over a low heat for another 30 minutes or so, until done.
5 Now carefully lift the plate of fish from the pan and pour off the liquid.
6 Serve the rice piled onto a platter and hand round the fish separately.

TIP: Fried eggs go very well with this dish.

QALIEH MAHI

STEAMED FISH FROM THE SOUTH

SERVES 4

800g (1lb 12oz) fish fillets (sea bass or another
    firm-fleshed fish)

salt, pepper

1 bulb garlic

1 onion

1 tablespoon tamarind paste

oil

2 tablespoons flour

1 teaspoon turmeric

1 pinch sugar

1–2 teaspoons hot red paprika

large bunch (sufficient to fill 1 good cup when
    chopped) fresh coriander

1–2 tablespoons dried fenugreek leaves

1 Salt the fish fillets.

2 Finely chop the garlic and onion. Pour 750ml (27fl oz)
water in a bowl and dissolve the tamarind paste in it.

3 Heat a little oil in a large pan and fry the onion over a
medium heat until it is golden. Sprinkle the flour over the
onion and sweat it briefly until golden, stirring two or
three times.

4 Add the garlic, season with the turmeric, sugar and
paprika, and stir three or four times.

5 De-stalk the coriander and chop the leaves. Add the
leaves and dried fenugreek to the pan and sweat everything
over a low heat until the moisture has evaporated and an
aromatic scent of herbs rises.

6 Lay the raw fish fillets on the herb and onion mixture
and add the tamarind water; bring everything to the boil
and reduce the heat to low.

7 Cover the pan and cook gently for about 30 minutes.
Season generously to taste with salt and pepper.

8 Serve with rice or bread.

NOTE: This is a famous dish from Bushehr, and is one
of the few original Persian fish dishes in which the fish
is not simply pan-fried.

VARIATION: In Khoramshahr on the Persian Gulf, the
fish is first fried with the onions. The remaining ingredients are then added, together with the water. In addition,
1–2 halved, de-seeded dried limes are added to the fish.

Below and right: Persian cuisine has its fair share
of special fish dishes.

KUFTEH TABRIZI
STUFFED DUMPLINGS FROM TABRIZ

SERVES 4

80g (30g) *lapeh* (yellow lentils)

150g (5¹/₂oz) rice

salt, pepper

300g (10¹/₂oz) spring onions (scallions), chopped

2 tablespoons barberries

5 tablespoons finely chopped fresh tarragon (or
  2 tablespoons chopped dried tarragon)

500g (1lb 2oz) minced (ground) beef

¹/₂ teaspoon saffron, ground

1–2 eggs (as required)

10–12 *alu* (yellow prunes – available in Persian shops)

2–3 tablespoons walnut kernels, finely chopped

2 onions

oil

1 teaspoon turmeric

2–3 tablespoons sumac (optional — *see* Tip)

1 Wash the *lapeh* (yellow lentils), pour over boiling water to cover, and let soak overnight. The next day, drain in a sieve and rinse with fresh water. Cook for 30 minutes in a saucepan in plenty of unsalted water, then drain.

2 Wash the rice and soak in fresh water for 1 hour. Cook in boiling salted water for 4–7 minutes, until it tests *al dente*. Drain in a sieve and leave to cool.

3 Wash the spring onions; trim off the top two-thirds and finely chop the white parts.

4 Tip the dried barberries onto a flat plate and sort through them, discarding any small stones. Rinse them in a sieve under cold water and drain well.

5 Place the spring onions, tarragon, *lapeh* and minced beef in a large bowl and knead until thoroughly mixed.

6 When everything is well-combined, add the rice and saffron and season with salt and pepper. Continue kneading until you have a homogeneous mixture. The final mixture should be sticky enough to hold together when rolled into balls, so start off by adding 1 egg and mixing well. Work in a second egg if necessary, without allowing the mixture to become too soft.

7 Now roll the mixture into good-sized balls (a little smaller than a tennis ball). As they are to be stuffed, take half the quantity of one ball in the palm of your hand, press the mixture flat, and place a prune, some of the chopped walnuts and a few barberries in the hollow.

8 Next, place the other half of the meatball mixture on top and shape gently by rolling between the palms of your hands into a nice, firm dumpling (this is most easily done with moistened hands, so dip your hands in a bowl of cold water from time to time). The stuffing should be completely enclosed by the meat mixture.

9 Finely chop the onions. Heat some oil in a large pan and fry over a moderate heat until golden. Sprinkle with turmeric and stir once. Pour in 1 litre (35fl oz) hot water and bring everything to the boil.

10 Carefully slide the dumplings into the gently boiling water, cover, and simmer over a low-to-moderate heat for 1¹/₄ hours. At the end of the cooking time there should be just 250-500ml (9-18fl oz) of sauce left in the pan, so towards the end, leave the lid open a little if necessary to allow any excess liquid to evaporate.

11 To serve, carefully lift the dumplings from the pan and arrange in an attractive deep bowl. Spoon just a little sauce over them, and hand round the remaining sauce in a gravy boat.

TIP: Before serving, sprinkle another 2–3 tablespoons sumac over the *kufteh* – this is a particular personal favourite of mine. Serve with fresh flatbread.

VARIATION: Shortly before the onions turn golden, sprinkle 1 tablespoon dried mint into the pan and stir once, then add the turmeric and stir again. Pour over the water and proceed as described above. The *kufteh* will be even more savoury and fragrant!

BAQALA QATOQ
BROAD (FAVA) BEANS WITH EGG

SERVES 4

180g (6¹/₄oz) dried broad (fava) beans (*baqali*)
4 garlic cloves
large bunch (sufficient to fill ¹/₂ cup when
   chopped) fresh dill
100g (3¹/₂oz) butter
¹/₂ teaspoon turmeric
5 eggs
salt, pepper

1 The day before you intend to serve the dish, sort through and wash the beans and soak them overnight in cold water. The next day, rinse in a sieve and drain well.
2 Chop the garlic very finely. Wash the dill and remove the stalks, then finely chop the tips.
3 Heat the butter in a large pan and stir-fry the beans, dill, garlic and turmeric over a moderate heat, taking care not to let anything burn.
4 As soon as the ingredients are slightly browned, pour in just enough water to cover about 250ml (9fl oz) and stir once.
5 Cover the pan and simmer for about 40–50 minutes. The beans should be done, but still retain some 'bite'. The water should not be allowed to evaporate completely: top up occasionally with a little hot water, if needed, so that nothing burns.
6 Shortly before serving, crack the eggs into the pan but do not stir. Cook, covered, over a low heat for a further 5–10 minutes, until the eggs have set.
7 Season generously to taste with salt and pepper before serving.

TIP: This is a typical dish from the north. Serve with pan-fried or smoked fish, rice (*kateh*), pickled olives, yogurt and fresh radishes.

Clockwise from top left: Rug dealer in the Tabriz bazaar; in a tea-house under a bridge in Isfahan; courting couple at the Hafez Mausoleum; woman knotting a rug in Nain.

KHORESHT-E KADU-YE TANBAL

PUMPKIN STEW

SERVES 8–10

70g (2¹/₂oz) *lapeh* (yellow lentils)

2 large onions, peeled

500g (1lb 2oz) minced (ground) lamb

1 tablespoon flour

salt, pepper

clarified butter

1kg (2lb 4oz) Hokkaido pumpkin (or butternut squash)

500g (1lb 2oz) lamb shoulder, very finely cubed

1 teaspoon saffron, ground

¹/₂ teaspoon each cinnamon, cardamom, ginger and
   ground black pepper

1 clove, pounded in a mortar

5 garlic cloves, finely chopped

2 tablespoons dried mint

6 tablespoons Greek yogurt with 10 per cent fat, or *kashk*

salt, pepper

1 The day before you intend to serve the dish, wash the *lapeh* (yellow lentils) and leave to soak overnight. The next day, drain in a sieve and rinse. Cook the *lapeh* in plenty of boiling, unsalted water for about 30 minutes.

2 Finely grate 1 onion. Coarsely chop the other onion and set aside.

3 Place the minced lamb in a large bowl and add the grated onion. Sprinkle over the flour, season generously, and mix everything together well with your fingers.

4 Roll the meat mixture into balls about the size of a table-tennis ball, moistening your hands repeatedly in a bowl of cold water to prevent sticking.

5 Heat 1 tablespoon clarified butter in a large, deep non-stick pan. Add the meatballs and brown them all over, then remove them, cover and set aside.

6 Peel the pumpkin and cut it into medium-sized (3cm/1¹/₄-inch) chunks. Bring a large panful of water to the boil and add the pumpkin and 1 teaspoon salt. As soon as the water comes back to a rolling boil, drain the pumpkin in a sieve.

7 Heat a little clarified butter in a large pan. Add the drained pumpkin and fry on medium-to-high heat for 6–7 minutes, then cover and set aside.

8 Heat the remaining clarified butter in the large pan in which you browned the meatballs. Add the chopped onion and fry until golden. Add the cubed lamb shoulder and continue frying until the meat is light brown. Add the saffron, cinnamon, cardamom, ginger, pepper and pounded clove to the meat and stir.

9 Pour over 500ml (18fl oz) water, cover, and simmer over a low-to-medium heat for 1 hour. Check occasionally that there is enough liquid in the pan and that the ingredients are not threatening to stick or burn, adding a few tablespoonfuls of boiling water one at a time as necessary.

10 Now add the boiled *lapeh*, if necessary pouring in a little hot water so that nothing burns, cover, and continue simmering over a low heat for 1 hour.

11 If you are using the *kashk*, mix 6–8 tablespoons with 250ml (9fl oz) water in a small saucepan and cook uncovered for 20 minutes, stirring, then set aside.

12 Add the pumpkin and meatballs to the large pan with the *lapeh*, adding a little hot water if necessary, cover, and simmer over a low heat for another hour at least. If the *khoresh* is too soupy, let it simmer uncovered for a few minutes to reduce the excess liquid – only about 250ml (9fl oz) liquid should remain at the end.

13 Heat a little oil in a small pan and fry the chopped garlic until golden.

14 Sprinkle in the mint and stir very briefly, until the fragrance rises, then decant into a small bowl (the mint will take on a bitter taste if allowed to get too dark).

15 Pour enough *kashk* or yogurt into a large bowl to generously cover the bottom. Using a skimmer, spread the solid ingredients of the *khoresh* over the top. Now carefully pour over the sauce and cover with the remaining *kashk* or yogurt.

16 Decorate the *khoresh* with the garlic-mint mixture.

NOTE: This dish, handed down from the cuisine of the Safavid court, can be served either with fresh flatbread or with rice (*chelo*).

Left: The barren landscape is relieved only by the green of the oases; often, vehicles with their loads provide the sole splashes of colour.

BERYAN GUSFAND
ROAST LAMB SAFAVID STYLE

SERVES 8–10

1 leg of lamb

2 large onions

2 cinnamon sticks

salt, pepper

1 teaspoon saffron, ground

4 tablespoons butter

YOU WILL ALSO NEED:

8–10 servings of rice (*chelo*), *see* **recipe page 72**
(adjust quantities)

500ml (18fl oz) yogurt

1 Place the lamb in a large pan with the whole peeled onions and cinnamon sticks. Pour in enough water to cover and season with salt and pepper. Cover and simmer for 2 hours.

2 While the lamb is cooking, wash the rice and soak in cold water to which 1 tablespoon salt has been added.

3 Preheat the oven to 200°C/400°F/gas mark 6. Put the rice on to cook.

4 As soon as the rice is steaming in the pan, dissolve the saffron in 4 tablespoons hot water. Remove the cooked meat from the pan and place in a deep baking tin or a large roasting tray. Brush with butter and the saffron water and season generously with salt and pepper.

5 Roast the lamb for an hour or so, basting frequently with its own juices (from the pan) so that it does not dry out.

6 To serve, carve the meat from the bone and place on a platter. Serve with rice (*chelo*) and yogurt.

TIP: A pressure cooker is ideal for boiling the meat – the cooking time is reduced (check cooking times) and the flavour is nicely preserved.

NOTE: The unusual feature of this Safavid dish is that the meat is first boiled, then roasted.

CHALOQMEH
SAFAVID-STYLE SAVOURY PASTRIES

SERVES 4–6

1 medium onion

oil

1/2 teaspoon turmeric

500g (1lb 2oz) minced (ground) beef

1/2 teaspoon each nutmeg, black pepper, paprika and salt

1 teaspoon butter

burek pastry (available in chilled-foods in Greek or
  Middle-Eastern stores), or use frozen filo or puff pastry

a little melted butter for brushing

1–2 tablespoons icing sugar

1 teaspoon ground cinnamon

1 teaspoon dried rose petals (optional; available from
  Persian shops)

1 Finely chop the onion. Heat a little oil in a large pan and fry until golden. Sprinkle with turmeric and stir.

2 Add the meat and fry until brown, stirring frequently. Add the nutmeg, pepper, paprika, salt and 1 teaspoon butter to the meat and stir to combine. Remove the pan from the heat.

3 Preheat the oven to 200°C/400°F/gas mark 6.

4 Lay the pastry out flat on a chopping board (rolling it out if necessary) and cut into 10cm (4-inch) squares. Place 1–2 tablespoons of the meat mixture in the centre of each square of pastry and fold into triangles, pressing the edges together tightly to seal.

5 Place the pastry triangles on a baking sheet lined with waxed paper, brush with melted butter, and bake in the preheated oven for about 45 minutes.

6 Dust the finished turnovers sparingly with a mixture of icing sugar and cinnamon. Crush the rose petals to a powder between your fingers and sprinkle over the top. Serve hot.

NAN-E BARBARI

THICK FLATBREAD

MAKES 4 FLATBREADS

750g (1lb 10oz) flour

15g (¹/₂oz) fresh yeast or 7g (¹/₄oz) dried yeast

¹/₄ teaspoon sugar

2 teaspoons salt

2 tablespoons oil

sesame seeds and/or black onion seeds, optional

1 Pour the flour into a large plastic bowl and make a well in the centre. Dissolve the yeast in 50ml (2fl oz) lukewarm water and leave for 10 minutes. Now add 280ml (9¹/₂fl oz) water along with the sugar, salt, oil and dissolved yeast to the flour, kneading all the ingredients for about 10 minutes, until you have a very soft dough. Add a little more warm water if the dough is too dry.

2 Shape the dough into a large ball, cover, and leave to rise in a warm place for about 1¹/₂ hours.

3 Line a baking sheet with waxed paper. Shape the dough into 4 balls and, with a rolling pin, roll out into ovals about 1cm (¹/₂-inch) thick. Make a few indentations in the dough with your fingertips. Sprinkle a little warm water over the flatbreads, cover, and leave for another 20 minutes.

4 Preheat the oven to a good 240°C/475°F/gas mark 9.

5 Sprinkle the flatbreads with sesame seeds and/or black onion seeds, and bake for 15–20 minutes in the centre of the oven.

TIP: Place a small baking dish containing hot water at the bottom of the oven. The steam will give the flatbreads a nice crumb.

NAN-E SAJI

PAN-BAKED FLATBREAD

MAKES 6–8 FLATBREADS

380g (13¼oz) flour
1 tablespoon oil
½ teaspoon salt
1 generous pinch sugar
1 teaspoon aniseed (optional)

1 Place the flour in a large plastic bowl. Add the oil, salt and sugar, and pour in 280ml (10fl oz) lukewarm water.
2 Knead all the ingredients thoroughly by hand for about 10 minutes, until you have a soft, supple dough, adding a couple of tablespoons of lukewarm water if necessary.
3 Shape the dough into a ball, cover, and let rest in a warm place for 30 minutes.
4 Divide the dough into 6–8 portions. Roll each portion out as thinly as possible, to fit the size of the pan.

5 Heat a heavy, flat pan – use a cast-iron pan if possible. Place one flatbread in the hot pan and cook for around 2–3 minutes. Press the flatbread here and there with a wooden spoon or similar flat tool, then flip over and cook on the other side.
6 Wrap the cooked flatbreads in a slightly damp, clean tea towel, which will help them to keep soft until ready to be served.

TIP: You can sprinkle aniseed over the flatbreads before cooking if you prefer.

Left and below: nan-e sangak – the daily bread of many Iranians – is baked fresh every day on the hot pebbles of the floor of a simple oven.

SWEETS AND DRINKS

SHIRINI VA NUSHABEH

Anyone tasting Persian sweets for the first time will be surprised by their subtle and refined flavour. Persian sweets are a whole world in themselves, with their own importance; ideal served as a dessert, these choice, sophisticated nibbles are equally suitable at a tea party.

In Iran, pastries and sweets are not only – and not even predominantly – served as a pudding. Just as Persian cooking in general follows no set sequence of courses, there is no automatic expectation of a sweet finale after *polo*, *khorak* or *kebab*. It might well be on the cards, and it's always welcome, but *sholeh zard* (saffron rice) or *fereni* (rice pudding) are also enjoyed as a between-meals snack. This is even truer for *halva* or *nokhodchi*, which are usually consumed with a cup of tea and frequently offered to guests. In general, guests are never left sitting without something to eat. Sweetmeats are naturally laid on when there are visitors, but there is always also *miveh*: ripe, delicious seasonal fruit.

When visitors are expected, it is usual to buy fresh pastries from the cake shop, where the choice, ranging from multi-layered cream slices and crisp, airy puff pastries to the most delicate biscuits, is truly wide and tempting. So too are the bold wedding cakes, for which every Persian pastry shop has its own specific thick book on display, from which one's heart's desire may be chosen from among hundreds of models in every imaginable style. Some are truly amazing works of art, with intricate buttercream ruffles and a riot of colourful marzipan flowers. And if the sought-after model is not there, a towering cake can be made to order – five tiers tends to be the minimum – and the fanciest wishes catered to. Persian pastry chefs rightly see themselves as artists. Among all the opulence, however, the basic tenet of Persian cookery also applies for the Persian pastry-cook: treat your guest like royalty!

Persian baking is what it is because of the delicate scent of its ingredients: pistachios, almonds, walnuts, cardamom, honey, rose-water and saffron. The same is also true for homemade Persian desserts. The oriental art of flattering the palate should not be underestimated, however. The subtle flavours of these delicacies are achieved by the use of potent, concentrated ingredients.

During the meal, water or *dugh* (yogurt with mint, thinned down with water), and occasionally wine are drunk. Strangely enough, wine does not go particularly well with Persian food. Many like the combination, but moderation seems to improve the meal. The scent of Persian foods is a world that only rarely harmonizes with the bouquet of the wine. *Dugh*, on the other hand, whether drunk plain or flavoured with herbs, goes dazzlingly well with Persian food. It's also an outstanding thirst-quencher, and extremely invigorating. Fresh lemonade or freshly squeezed fruit juices are also a boon in summer, and truly delectable when the different varieties of melon are in season.

Tea is enjoyed on all occasions, but although it plays a definite role in the social round, it is not viewed as a thirst-quencher, served as it is in small, delicate glasses rather than in cups or large mugs. There are different kinds of sugar that are enjoyed with tea, from small white sugars that look like candy and taste of rose-water, to rock sugar, boiled with saffron, giving it a brilliant yellow colour. In addition, there are crunchy sugar-coated almonds, or caramel croquants – with and without nuts – and white nougat, the confectionery Persians call 'Turkish honey'. Soft, fleshy, highly aromatic Persian dates are also a popular snack with tea, and, of course, a healthy one.

Black tea is ubiquitous in Iran, and an essential accompaniment throughout the day. Simmering away gently in the background, the samovar is an unobtrusive reminder of its ready generosity. Whether to accompany a quiet moment of leisure or a sociable chat, there's always time for a small glass of strong *chay* (tea) to invigorate mind and body. And more often than not, the glass of tea stimulates the thought that perhaps a little sweetmeat wouldn't be out of place.

SHOLEH ZARD

SAFFRON RICE

شله زرد

SERVES 8

250g (9oz) rice
1/2 teaspoon saffron, ground
50g (1³/4oz) flaked/slivered almonds
150g (5¹/2oz) sugar
50g (1³/4oz) butter
125ml (4fl oz) rose-water
1/2 teaspoon cinnamon
a few pistachios

1 Wash the rice and put it in a large pan with 1.5 litres (55fl oz) of water. Place over a high heat and as soon as the rice has come to the boil, skim off any froth and reduce the heat to a simmer.
2 After 15 minutes, add half the saffron and all of the almonds to the rice. Drizzle in the sugar, stirring. Sprinkle in the remaining saffron, add the butter, and stir gently to combine. Add 125ml (4fl oz) water if needed.
3 Pour in the rose-water and continue stirring. If the rice

mixture has become very solid, add enough boiling water to return it to a syrupy consistency. The mixture should be fairly firm by now, though, and a spoonful ladled onto a plate should not run.
4 Cover the pan and cook the *sholeh zard* for 1 hour over the lowest possible heat, removing the lid for the final 20 minutes of cooking so that the excess moisture can evaporate and the golden saffron rice acquires a pudding-like consistency.
5 Ladle the saffron rice into small bowls. As soon as it cools, decorate with ground cinnamon and pistachios and serve.

NOTE: *Sholeh zard* (*see* the photograph, opposite) is a delicate, fragrant rice pudding whose secret lies in the addition of rose-water and saffron. It is prepared on festive occasions and distributed to friends on religious holidays. There are many variations of this recipe. My recipe is not overly sweet, and should appeal to the European palate.

FERENI

RICE PUDDING

فرنی

SERVES 4

500ml (18fl oz) milk
50g (1³/4oz) rice flour
75g (2³/4oz) sugar
2 tablespoons rose-water

FOR THE DECORATION:
1/2 teaspoon ground cinnamon
dried rose petals
pistachios, shelled and chopped

1 In a saucepan, beat together a little of the milk with 1 teaspoon of the rice flour. Gradually add the remaining milk and rice flour, beating until smooth.
2 Place the saucepan over a moderate heat and bring the mixture to a boil.

3 Reduce heat to the lowest setting and remove the saucepan from the heat.
4 Pour in the sugar in a thin trickle and stir until it dissolves. Place the pan back on the heat and cook the *fereni* on the lowest setting for 30 minutes, stirring, until thickened and creamy.
5 Add the rose-water and simmer the rice for a further 5 minutes, stirring constantly. Raise the heat slightly if necessary, but keep stirring so that the mixture does not catch and burn.
6 Ladle the *fereni* into individual dessert bowls or a larger presentation bowl and allow it to cool. Dust lightly with cinnamon and serve garnished with the rose petals and pistachios.

ZULBIA

SYRUP SPIRALS

دولبیا

MAKES ABOUT 30–40 SPIRALS

FOR THE BATTER:

500g (1lb 2oz) potato starch
60g (2¹/₄oz) flour
¹/₂ teaspoon bicarbonate of soda
¹/₄ teaspoon saffron, ground
500ml (18fl oz) yogurt
125ml (4fl oz) sour cream
oil for deep frying

FOR THE SYRUP:

1.2kg (2lb 11oz) sugar
1 lemon
4 tablespoons rose-water
1 teaspoon ground cardamom

1 In a large bowl, carefully mix the potato starch with
the flour and bicarbonate of soda.
2 Dissolve the saffron in 1–2 tablespoons hot water.
Once it has cooled, mix it with the yogurt in a small bowl
until thoroughly blended.
3 Add the saffron yogurt to the flour mixture, followed
by the sour cream, and blend everything with a hand
mixer to a thick, creamy, slightly stiff batter.
4 Cover the batter and allow it to rest at room
temperature for 3 hours.
5 To make the syrup, bring 500ml (18fl oz) water and the
sugar to the boil in a wide pan. Squeeze the lemon, then
add the lemon juice, the rose-water and cardamom to the
boiling water and simmer all the ingredients uncovered at
a low to moderate heat, or until the liquid is syrupy,
stirring frequently.
6 Keep the syrup warm over a low heat (do not allow it
to get cold, or it will become solid).
7 Heat oil to a depth of at least 2cm (³/₄-inch) in a large,
wide pan (or wok). As soon as the oil has reached the
correct temperature (when tiny bubbles cluster around a
wooden toothpick held in the oil), reduce the heat slightly
and pour some of the batter into a pastry bag with a thin
(0.5cm/¹/₄-inch) nozzle.

8 Pipe the batter in spiral shapes into the hot oil, beginning at the centre and looping around 3 times in a circle,
then finishing with half a figure 8 over the entire spiral
to create a pretzel-like effect. Depending on the size of the
pan, you may be able to pipe several spirals side-by-side
into the hot oil, but do not let them touch or they will
stick together.
9 As soon as a spiral is golden on one side, turn it over
carefully with two forks and fry until the other side is
golden as well.
10 Once they are done, lift out the spirals with a slotted
spoon, holding them briefly over a plate lined with paper
towels to catch the excess oil, and, while still hot, dip
them very quickly in the syrup.
11 Stack the *zulbia* on an attractive serving plate.

TIP: If there are two of you to make *zulbia*, the task is
easier: one person watches the spirals as they cook in the
oil, the other fills the pastry bag and dips the finished *zulbia* into the syrup. *Zulbia* are a delectable snack, and taste
especially good freshly fried with a glass of tea.
They are also great to bring along to a party.

Page 156-157: Five of the eleven bridges of Isfahan
were erected by Shah Abbas in the 17th century.

NOCHODCHI

CHICKPEA FLOUR BISCUITS

MAKES ABOUT 50 BISCUITS
150g (5¹/₂oz) butter
150g (5¹/₂oz) icing sugar
300g (10¹/₂oz) chickpea flour
¹/₂ teaspoon ground cardamom
100g (3¹/₂oz) pistachios, flaked

1 Melt the butter in a large, wide pan over a low heat. It should just liquefy, without getting hot.
2 Sieve the icing sugar into the melted butter and stir until completely dissolved.
3 Mix the chickpea flour with the cardamom and gradually sieve into the butter and sugar mixture. Knead everything until thoroughly combined.

4 Shape the dough into a ball, cover, and allow it to rest for 6 hours.
5 Preheat the oven to 150°C/300°F/gas mark 2.
6 Roll out the dough on waxed paper to a thickness of about 0.5cm (¹/₄-inch). Cut out with very small biscuit cutters (round or clover-shaped) and press a flaked pistachio into each biscuit.
7 Bake the *nochodchi* for about 10–15 minutes in the preheated oven until pale golden in colour, taking care not to let them get too dark.
8 Allow the biscuits to cool, and store them in a biscuit tin for maximum freshness.

HALVA

BUTTER CONFECTIONERY

100g (3¹/₂oz) flour
100g (3¹/₂oz) butter
¹/₂ teaspoon saffron, ground
100g (3¹/₂oz) sugar
¹/₂ teaspoon cardamom, ground
3 tablespoons rose-water
100g (3¹/₂oz) flaked coconut

1 Dry-roast the flour in a high-sided pan over a low heat for 5 minutes, stirring constantly; it should turn dark yellow to light brown in colour.
2 Add the butter and very gently brown the mixture over the lowest heat for 20 minutes, stirring constantly (take care – the flour must not be allowed to burn), then tip into a bowl.

3 Bring 100ml (3¹/₂fl oz) water to the boil in a pan. Add the saffron, sugar, cardamom and rose-water and stir until the sugar dissolves. Now gradually stir this hot liquid into the bowl with the flour. The mixture should turn creamy. If necessary, add a little more water.
4 Spread the mixture onto a flat plate, or shape into flat, oval biscuits.
5 Sprinkle the flaked coconut decoratively over the *halva*, and cut on the diagonal into diamond shapes.

TIP: The *halva* is also good sprinkled with chopped pistachios.

FROM THE RUBAIYAT OF OMAR KHAYYAM

گویند مرا که دوزخی باشد مست

قولی است خالف و دل بر آن نتوان بست

گر عاشق و میخواره بدوزخ باشد

فردا بینی بهشت چون کف دست

Guyand ma-ra ke duzakhi bashad mast

Qoul ast khalef o del bar an natavan bast

Gar 'asheq o meykhareh be duzakh bashad

Farda bini behesht chun kaf-e dast

If but the Wine- and Love-abjuring Band

Are in the Prophet's Paradise to stand,

Alack, I doubt the Prophet's Paradise

Were empty as the hollow of one's Hand.

Omar Khayyam: Rubaiyat, Tehran, 1867 and many further editions.
Translation by Edward Fitzgerald.

KACHI
SAFFRON PUDDING

SERVES 8

150g (5¹/₂oz) butter

200g (7oz) flour

200g (7oz) sugar

1 teaspoon saffron, ground

1 teaspoon cinnamon

¹/₂ teaspoon ground cardamom

4 tablespoons rose-water

8 tablespoons pistachios, chopped (for garnishing)

1 Melt the butter in a large pan over a medium heat. Gradually add the flour, stirring constantly. Cook the mixture for about 15 minutes, stirring, until light brown.

2 Pour in about 900ml (32fl oz) water, stir in the sugar, and let everything come to the boil.

3 In a separate small pan, bring 100ml (3¹/₂fl oz) water to the boil. Add the saffron, cinnamon and cardamom, and, once they have dissolved, pour in the rose-water.

4 Now stir everything into the flour mixture. Simmer for a few minutes over a low heat, until the mixture is thick and creamy.

5 To serve, spoon the pudding into small bowls and sprinkle with the chopped pistachios.

NOTE: This substantial dessert is served warm. It may taste a little unusual to the European palate. You can stir in a little yogurt if you like, and hand around fresh fruit as an accompaniment.

MORABBA-YE ZERESHK
BARBERRY JAM

MAKES 3 SMALL JARS

250g (9oz) dried barberries

500ml (18fl oz) apple juice (cloudy)

1 cinnamon stick

4 green cardamom pods

4 saffron threads

200g (7oz) preserving sugar

1 Carefully sort through the barberries, discarding any small stones, then wash them and drain them well.

2 Put the drained berries in a bowl, pour over the apple juice, cover, and refrigerate for at least 4 hours (or preferably overnight).

3 Transfer the barberries with the apple juice to a large pan (to prevent the mixture from boiling over as it cooks). Add the cinnamon stick, cardamom pods and saffron threads, and bring everything to the boil over a high heat, stirring continously.

4 Now quickly drizzle in all the preserving sugar while still stirring.

5 Cook the mixture at a rolling boil for exactly 4 minutes, stirring continuously.

6 Remove the cinnamon stick and cardamom pods and pour the hot jam into clean jars that have been sterilized with boiling water, then dried.

7 Seal the jars immediately.

Right: Persian saffron is reputed to be the best in the world, and is expensive even in the bazaars of Iran.

Following pages: On the road to Yazd.

SHARBAT-E ABLIMU
FRESH LEMONADE

شربت آبلیمو

SERVES 4

3 large lemons (or 5 limes) with unwaxed skins
1–2 tablespoons sugar (to taste)
ice cubes (optional)

1 Squeeze the lemons or limes, keeping one aside for garnish. Pour the juice into a glass carafe, stir in the sugar and pour in 1 litre (35fl oz) cold water.
2 Wash the remaining lemon (or lime) in hot water and cut into very thin slices. Add ice-cubes and the lemon or lime slices to the jug and serve.

NOTE: In Iran, it is popular to substitute limes for lemons when making this drink. Lime juice has an even fresher and more intense flavour. The fruit can also be mixed, and half a lemon and half a lime cut into thin slices and added to the carafe. In summer, no drink is more refreshing.

DUGH
YOGURT DRINK

دوغ

SERVES 6–8

500ml (18fl oz) yogurt
1.5 litres (53fl oz) water
2 tablespoons dried mint
salt

1 Whisk 3 tablespoons of the yogurt and 3 tablespoons of water together in a jug or carafe until smooth. Add the mint and beat in the remaining yogurt and 1.5 litres (53fl oz) water gradually, so no lumps form. Season to taste with salt.

TIP: Fresh mint can, of course, also be used. Wash and shake dry the mint, and very finely chop the leaves only, discarding the stalks. Fresh mint should be stirred in just before serving. If you wish, a dash of lemon juice can also be added.

NOTE: *Dugh* is wonderfully refreshing, and an effective pick-me-up. In Iran, *dugh* is sometimes also seasoned with thyme (*kukati*) or oregano (*puneh*) and salted to taste. The ratio of yogurt to water is always about 1:3.

PALUDE
MELON JUICE

پالوده

SERVES 4

1 ripe honeydew melon
1 lemon
2 tablespoons sugar
ice-cubes
1 sprig fresh mint (optional)

1 Halve and de-seed the melon. Cut out and quarter a narrow sliver for the garnish. Scoop the flesh out of both halves with a spoon and transfer to a blender.

2 Squeeze the lemon. Sprinkle the sugar onto a flat plate. Using tall, thin-walled glasses if possible, dip the rim of the glasses first in the lemon juice, then in the sugar, to create a pretty frosted edge.
3 Coarsely crush the ice-cubes in a clean tea towel with a small hammer and add to the melon flesh in the blender. Blend thoroughly and carefully pour into the frosted glasses. Place a piece of melon and a mint leaf on the rim of the glass (or spear on a cocktail stick) and serve immediately.

CHAY
TEA

SERVES 4

½ cinnamon stick
4 green cardamom pods
4 teaspoons strong black tea-leaves, *e.g.* **Assam**

1 Cut the cinnamon stick into two pieces. Coarsely pound the whole cardamom pods in a mortar with a pestle, so that the flavour can develop more fully.
2 Place the tea-leaves and spices in a teapot and pour over 600ml (20fl oz) boiling water. Let the tea brew for 3–5 minutes, according to taste.

TIP: Persian *rand* (sugar cubes) are much firmer in consistency than those we are used to, which is why they do not dissolve so quickly in the mouth. If you are not able to get hold of any Iranian sugar, look out for a Continental-style sugar pyramid, which can be wrapped in a tea towel and crushed into sugar-cube-sized pieces with a small hammer.

NOTE: Black tea is a ubiquitous beverage in Iran, and an indispensable part of any gathering, be it business or private. It is traditionally drunk from d inty glasses.

Different types of sugar are served with tea in Iran. There is white rock sugar, and even a sugar that is flavoured with rose water, which lends a fine fragrance to the tea.

Sugar cubes are either dissolved in the tea or placed directly on the tongue, where they dissolve as the hot tea is sipped.

It is also customary to serve fresh dates with tea in Iran. Persian dates are almost black, with a small stone surrounded by flesh that is so soft and sweet that they practically melt in the mouth.

The popular pastries that accompany tea include various kinds of biscuits, such as *nochodchi* (*see* page 158) or *zulbia* (*see* page 154), or little cakes and cream slices which are hardly ever made at home but bought fresh from the pastry shop.

VARIATIONS ON BLACK TEA:
Lime tea: Halve and de-seed a dried lime (*limu omani*) and either place it in a teapot with the tea-leaves and pour boiling water over both, or place a quarter of the lime in each teacup and fill the individual cups with the tea once brewed. You could also coarsely pound one (or more) green cardamom pod in a mortar and add to the pan.

Saffron tea: Add 4 saffron threads to the tea-leaves before pouring over the boiling water.

Tea with rose-water: Add 1 teaspoon dried rose petals to the tea-leaves, add boiling water and leave to infuse; before serving, add ¼ teaspoon rose water to the teapot.

Jasmine tea: Mix 3 teaspoons black tea with 1 teaspoon jasmine tea and add boiling water.

PREPARING TEA IN A SAMOVAR:
The advantage of using a samovar is that fresh black tea is constantly available, and can be brewed stronger or weaker for the person in question.

A samovar consists of 2 pots: the large one contains the hot water and the small one the tea. Boiling water from the large pot is poured over the leaves in the small pot and the tea is left to steep. The large pot sits over a source of heat or is heated electrically so that the water in it stays hot. The small pot sits like a lid on top of the large one, and the tea inside it is heated or kept warm via the rising steam.

To serve, the glasses are filled about one-third full with tea essence from the small pot, then topped up with water from the large pot. Before the small pot is replaced on top of the samovar, it is topped up with a few more tea-leaves and some boiling water from the large pot, along with a couple of cardamom pods and a cinnamon stick, according to taste.

Pages 170-171: Lake Bakhtegan (about 300km/ 185-miles east of Shiraz), with its high mineral content, has a wonderful natural beauty.

NORUZ

The biggest festival in the Persian calendar is the New Year's celebration, called *Eyd-e noruz*, the Festival of the New Day or New Light. Persians celebrate the new year at the beginning of spring, at the equinox on the 20th or 21st of March, when daylight gains the upper hand over darkness and nature is beginning to show the first signs of spring. This day is the first day of the first month of *Farvadin* (elections month) in the Persian year. All the months of the Persian year have Zoroastrian names, and the first day of *Farvadin* always falls on the 20th or 21st of March, as the Persian calendar, like the Christian one, is solar and there are 365 days in a year. For cultural and religious purposes, the Arabic–Islamic calendar, which is lunar and only has some 354 days in a year, is also used. The months of the lunar year, which are primarily important on account of the month of mourning of *Moharram* and the month of fasting, *Ramadan*, therefore cycle through the solar year, with each year being different by about eleven days (one extra in leap years). The Christian–European calendar is becoming increasingly important, too, making the keeping of a Persian appointments diary a task fraught with complexity.

There is, however, one fixed point in the year: *Noruz*, which to Iranians means roughly what Christmas means to Europeans. *Noruz* is the traditional high point of the year, a family festival with gift-giving galore, painted eggs, and thirteen days of holidays.

On the evening of the Wednesday before *Noruz*, festivities reach their first peak. Young people noisily roam the streets, with some of the boldest taking part in games of jumping over fire. They leap over the flames with cries of '*Sorkhi-e to az man, zardi-ye man az to*' ('Your redness is now mine, and my paleness yours!').

The real climax of the festivities, however, is *Saat-e tahvil*, the hour of the equinox. The whole family gathers to watch the countdown on television, and when the magic moment arrives, they throw their arms around each other and shout '*Eyd-e shoma mobarak*' and '*Sal-e no mobarak*' ('Best wishes for the new year!'). The sitting room has already been festively decorated with the *sofreh-ye haft sin* (the 'tablecloth with the seven S's'). These are seven items that all begin with the letter 's': *sabzi* (greens, usually a little 'meadow' of wheat-, barley- and lentil-sprouts sown in a bowl about 2 weeks beforehand); *sepand* (wild rue); *sib*

(apple); *sekkeh* (newly minted coins); *sir* (garlic); *s, rkeh* (vinegar) and *samanu* (wheat pudding).

Nowadays, as this is the start of the season of new growth, the Iranians do not stop at these seven items, but add *sangak* (bread), *somaq* (sumac), *sonbol* (hyacinths), and much more. Everything is carefully arranged in front of a mirror and 2 candlesticks, with a copy of the Koran, or the poet Ferdousi's *Shahnameh*, or Hafez's *Divan* placed on a nearby table. A bowl with one or 2 goldfish is often included. Although these are called *mahi*, so do not begin with the letter s, the goldfish are there as a reminder of the mythical giant *kara* fish, which dwells in the Vourukasha Sea and fends off all evil beings in the depths with its gimlet eyes. Everything on the *Sofreh-ye haft sin* table bears a deeper significance: growth, health, wealth, protection from all evil, and all the good and beautiful things that people hope for. Painted eggs also play an important part; they are a symbol of fertility, as they have been throughout the world since ancient times.

Families also look to their future wealth and prosperity, and it is the custom for adults to give younger members of the family a banknote, which often bears a hand-written dedication. The days that follow are made up of family visits and the exchange of hospitality, with food and meals naturally playing a central role. People also try to get away on holiday; half of Tehran crowds onto the arterial roads, and on the 13th day after *Noruz*, the last day of the holiday, it is no exaggeration to say that no one is left at home. On the pretext that the number thirteen brings bad luck, and that no one should therefore be at home on such a day, people head outdoors for a picnic. Iranians are enthusiastic picnickers, and will happily settle down on any small patch of green. Once a family has claimed its spot, the unpacking begins. The amount they bring with them almost defies description: a large tablecloth, towels and paper serviettes, plates, cutlery, glasses, baskets and cool-boxes with keys and more keys, pots containing delicacies of all kinds, pickled gherkins, bread and candy, a (large) gas cooker, board games, badminton equipment, Frisbees, and much, much more. Then they all settle down to eat and chat, putting aside all their cares and enjoying themselves immensely.

This is *Noruz* – a highly festive time that seems to combine minor chaos with peace and relaxation!

INGREDIENTS A TO Z

AUBERGINE (EGGPLANT) *(Bademjan)*
Medicinal value: warm, dry. Medieval Persian physicians unanimously warn about the aubergine's bitterness, although this can be neutralized by preparing the vegetable with oil or vinegar. The aubergine is then reputed to be beneficial in the treatment of bilious and auditory complaints.

The aubergine comes originally from India, to which its name still attests: from the Sanscrit *vatingana*, to the Persian *bademjan*, arabicized with the definite article to *al-badinjan*, from which the Catalan *alberginia* and French *aubergine* are derived. From India, the aubergine first became naturalized in Iran, arriving in the Mediterranean via trade with the Arabs. In Europe, the longish, dark-purple-to-black variety is the best-known. There are also brownish, purplish-red, egg-yolk-yellow, and nearly white varieties ranging from pea-sized to the size of a hen's egg – hence its other name 'eggplant' – and much larger.

Not every type of oil is suitable for frying aubergines. Groundnut oil or ghee (clarified butter) can both be heated to high temperatures, and are therefore recommended. It is a misconception that the less oil used in frying, the less oil the aubergines absorb. Just how much oil they sponge up depends primarily on how well they were salted beforehand and how long they were set aside to drain. Stinting with the oil when frying will simply give you aubergines that are black on the surface and raw inside. Ideally, you should use enough oil to come halfway up the slices. The oil should not smoke, yet it must be hot enough to impart a fine colour to the aubergines, and this temperature needs to be kept constant. If the oil is not hot enough, the aubergines will soak it up without cooking and browning. The result is a panful of pale-yellow to greenish aubergines with an unpleasant consistency and a bland taste. Frying aubergines requires patience. Even when the oil is hot, it takes quite a few minutes for the aubergines to become brown enough to require turning. It is not, however, advisable to leave the kitchen while they are cooking. Once the aubergines turn brown, they can burn very quickly.

Buying tip: aubergines should be as black as possible and be relatively soft to the touch. When pressed with a finger, the print should remain visible. Buy long, thin varieties.

BARBERRIES *(Zereshk or Barbari)*
Medicinal value: cold, dry. A remedy for biliousness; strengthens the stomach, liver and heart. The root contains berberine, an antibacterial alkaloid.

Barberry bushes grow in the northern, eastern and south-eastern highlands of Iran, but are also indigenous to Europe (usually as a decorative shrub). Summer sees the ripening of the red berries, whose juice is pleasantly tart. This relatively unknown fruit produces something that is far more interesting than lemon juice, and makes a good substitute for it in all recipes. The tart and bitter components, together with the fructose, impart an unmistakeable flavour to such dishes as *Zereshk polo*, and form an interesting contrast to oil, butter and meat wherever they are used.

In Persian literature, barberries (*zereshk*) are often compared with tears (*sereshk*), and in the cookery book of the culinary master Nurollah, chef to Shah Abbas I, *Zereshk polo* is actually written as *Sereshk polo*.

BARLEY *(Jo)*
Medicinal value: warm in the second degree.

Barley is used in the thick soup known as *ash*. Since the hull of the grain cannot be eaten, we must either resort to pearl barley (polished barley), of limited nutritional value since the mechanical hulling process also removes both the fibre-rich bran and the vitamin- and protein-rich germ, or pot barley, which is less refined. Another alternative is the relatively recent cultivar, the hull-less 'naked barley', which was known on Iranian soil as early as the 7th millennium BC and is nowadays available in the West in wholefood shops.

Left: Summer grain flourishes in the middle zones of the Zagros Mountains.

BEANS: BROAD (FAVA) *(Baqala, Baqali)*

Medicinal value: warm in the second degree; meant to strengthen bone marrow and brain, and to 'freshen' the blood.

Broad beans (*vicia faba*), also known as fava beans, are nowadays grown in Iran primarily in the Caspian regions. Found since ancient times throughout the Mediterranean and in the Near East, they have always been an important and popular staple food. Broad beans have a pleasantly nutty taste, and are a popular snack in the northern regions of Iran. They are delicious boiled, with a little salt and powdered marjoram (*puneh*).

In holiday locations, vendors sell fragrant bags of broad beans from stalls set up along the sea-front. The bean pods contain light-green beans that fall into two halves once they have undergone the obligatory shelling. Broad beans are available dried and ready-to-cook from Persian grocers.

BEANS: GREEN *(Lubia)*

Medicinal value: damp, and according to variety, cooling, or (in the case of the red varieties) warming.

The green bean (*Phaseolus vulgaris*), also known as the French bean, originated in South America and was brought by the Spanish conquistadors to Europe, from where it spread further afield to Asia.

Green beans are actually a colourful, widely ramified family of more or less related legumes (pulses). A few of the major varieties in Iran are *lubia chiti* (pinto beans) with a velvety pod and pink to reddish seeds; *lubia marmari* or *sefid* with white seeds; *lubia qermez* (kidney beans); *lubia taryaki*, opium-coloured beans; *lubia cheshm-bolboli* (nightingale's-eye beans), and *lubia siah-cheshm* (black-eyed beans): small and white with a black spot.

CARDAMOM *(Hel)*

Medicinal value: cardamom is 'warm and dry in the third degree. It warms, and acts as a styptic … with mastix and the juice of sweet and sour pomegranates, it helps against nausea and warms the stomach.' (Avicenna)

Green cardamom is a member of the ginger family. Its seeds, enclosed in a green pod, are used to spice sweet dishes such as *baqlava*, rice pudding or *zulbia*. Jams are also often enhanced with cardamom, and one or two cardamom pods will flavour black tea and revive the spirits.

CAVIAR *(Khaviar)*

Caviar is the unfertilized roe of the sturgeon. Three species of sturgeon are caught and reared for caviar production. They are best-known by their Russian names: *beluga* (Persian *fil-mahi*, or 'elephant fish'), *osetra* and *sevruga*. The eggs of the beluga sturgeon are the size of chickpeas, and a female may carry up to 20g (⅘oz) of roe. The eggs of the other species of sturgeon are smaller, and the yield per fish is lower.

Caviar has always been a luxury export. In Iran itself, its consumption was long prohibited, since the sturgeon was considered a scaleless fish, the eating of which was forbidden by the Koran. Recent Islamic research has shown, however, that the sturgeon does have microscopic scales. Ayatollah Khomeini personally stressed this in a legal opinion in 1983, and since then Iranians have been officially allowed to eat their own caviar.

CINNAMON *(Darchin)*

Medicinal value: relieves diarrhoea and flatulence, as well as fever and joint pain.

The dried and rolled bark of young branches of the Sri Lankan cinnamon tree is one of the oldest spices in existence. Cinnamon is referred to in China as far back as the third millennium BC, and in Egypt as early as the second millennium BC. Not to be confused with the lower-quality, sharper-tasting cassia bark, cinnamon is highly popular in Persian cuisine, used in discreet quantities.

CORIANDER *(Geshniz)*

Medicinal value: varies. Cold according to some, warm in the third degree according to others; good for flatulence and stomach upsets.

Coriander has enjoyed great popularity with Iranian peoples for many centuries. It has been found as a burial object in the Scythian tombs of the Altai region. Fresh green coriander is often used in herb mixtures for *ash*, *khoresh* and *kuku*, and is frequently included in the herb basket that forms part of every Persian meal.

Clockwise from top left: Freshly picked rose petals; dried limu omani; *spice mixture; pomegranate;* nabad *(rock sugar).*

CUMIN, CARAWAY (Zireh)

Medicinal value: cumin is warm, drying, astringent; it stimulates circulation and counteracts flatulence and stomach upsets.

The name *zireh* can be confusing, referring as it does to four different plant species: 'green' cumin (*Cuminum cyminum*); black cumin (*Bunium persicum*); caraway (*Carum carvi*); and nigella (*Nigella sativa*).

Common throughout Asia, cumin (*cuminum cyminum*) is only distantly related to the caraway of more northern climes (*Carum carvi*). Although the fruits of both plants (often referred to as 'seeds') resemble one another in their longish, slightly bowed shape, they taste quite different. In Iran and in India two varieties of cumin exist: 'green' cumin and black cumin, and these are closely related. When roasted, black cumin acquires a nutty taste.

Nigella is also sometimes misleadingly referred to as 'black cumin' or 'black onion seed', despite being related to neither. The seeds of the nigella plant (which, in this case, are true seeds) are pitch-black in colour and about the same size and shape as sesame seeds. The famous nigella or black seed oil is extracted from its seeds; it takes just a few drops of this very healthy, aromatic, and flavourful oil to add class to a salad dressing. Cumin was prized as a spice in Persia as far back as Safavid times. The cumin of Kerman is famous: a Persian figure of speech, *zireh be Kermän bordan* (to take cumin to Kerman) is equivalent to the British expression 'taking coals to Newcastle'.

DATES (Khorma)

Medicinal value: warm in the fourth degree.

An indigenous plant of Mesopotamia and Persia, the date-palm has been grown in that part of the world since time immemorial. Zoroastrians regarded the date-palm as one of the most valuable trees of all. Marco Polo reported extensive date plantations around Yazd, Kerman, and Hormuz, as a consequence of which the inhabitants of the south coast lived primarily on dates and salt fish. And as he himself remarked, date wine shoots powerfully into the blood. The date-palm has been celebrated in innumerable poems; some poets even speak of male and female date-palms capable of falling in love with one other.

Today, Iran is the biggest date producer in the world, exporting one million tonnes of the fruit in the year 2000. Dates are grown in all of the southernmost regions from the east to the west, and there are many different varieties of them. A high-fructose content means that dates keep for relatively long periods. Nevertheless, there are different

methods of preservation. Machine-harvested dates are dried. Fancier varieties of Persian dates are still sorted by hand and packed fresh in air-conditioned rooms. When buying, be aware of the difference; those who have once tasted Persian dates will be reluctant to go back to the machine-harvested, dry varieties.

DRINKING YOGURT (Dugh)
see YOGURT: DRINKING

FENUGREEK (Shanbalile)

Medicinal value: warm in the second degree. Anti-inflammatory and anti-pyretic; stimulates digestion and circulation. Dioskurides recommends mixing together nine pounds of fenugreek, five pounds of olive oil, one pound of calamus, and two pounds of Cyprus grass, leaving for one week, and then juicing the ingredients, in order to obtain a universal curative oil.

Fenugreek grows wild throughout the entire region between the Mediterranean and China. Cultivated as early as the first millennium BC in Assyria, in Egypt it was dedicated to the bull-god Apis, and remains of the plant were found in the tomb of Tutankhamen. Both the seeds and leaves are used. In central Europe, fenugreek is less well-known than its relative, sweet trefoil, whose leaves are used as a herb in Alpine cheeses. In Iran, fenugreek leaves are highly prized as an ingredient in different types of *khoresh*, particularly in *qormeh sabzi*. It resembles lovage in taste, but is somewhat stronger. Fenugreek leaves are available dried in Persian shops.

GARLIC (Sir), WILD GARLIC (Musir)

Medicinal value: warm in the fourth degree. Garlic powder is used in traditional medicine to treat skin diseases.

Garlic cloves should be halved after they are peeled: if there is a green shoot in the centre, always remove this before proceeding.

Wild garlic is grown and used in Iran primarily in the Caspian and Gulf regions. It is much milder and more digestible than the normal variety, and is available in a dried form at Persian grocers. The dried slices are soaked overnight in a small bowl of cold water, then chopped very finely and mixed with fresh yogurt and served as a side dish.

GRAPES (Angur), WINE (Sharab)
Medicinal value: cold and dry when unripe; warm when ripe.

Tradition has it that grapes were the first fruit eaten by Adam and Eve. The juice of unripe grapes (verjuice) is available in small bottles at Persian food shops; it can be replaced by freshly squeezed lemon juice, although this is slightly less sour.

Wine was known in Egypt and Mesopotamia as early as 3000 BC, and probably originated on the southern slopes of the Caucasus. According to one legend, the fermentation of grapes into wine was discovered at the court of the fabled first Persian king, Jamshid: King Jamshid loved grapes and therefore commanded that stocks be laid down for winter, by storing grapes in a large amphora. The stored grapes began to ferment, and since it was thought that they had become inedible, the contents of the amphora were labelled 'poison' and pushed into a remote corner. One day, a servant was suffering from such a terrible headache that she decided to end her life. She took some of the 'poison' – and to her surprise, did not die, but awoke after a soothing sleep, her headache completely vanished. This was immediately reported to the king, who richly rewarded the servant for her discovery, and was now able to pursue his love of grapes in yet another form. Ancient Greek and Roman authors were familiar with Persian wine, and even the Islamic conquest in the 7th century did not appreciably alter the drinking habits of the Persians. Arab and European travellers reported on drinking orgies at the Safavid court, and even the Islamic clergy was reputed not always to have been abstinent.

The wine trade, however, lay in Jewish and Christian hands. The international trade centre for wine was Shiraz, where in the 17th and 18th centuries, English, Dutch and Portuguese companies exported to the East Indies. The fame of this wine was proverbial. Travel guides as recently as the 1970s were recommending a wine-tasting on any visit to Shiraz as a 'must-do'. According to one theory, one of the oldest and most estimable grape varieties in the world, Syrah, which was cultivated in Provence in antiquity, derives its name from Shiraz. The Shiraz vines that have been cultivated in Australia over the last few decades are certainly named after the Persian city.

Only the 1979 Islamic Revolution put an official end to this time-honoured tradition. Christians and Jews are still permitted to make wine for their own consumption, however. Naturally there are still vines all over Iran, grown for the fresh grapes and to produce raisins and vinegar. Over the intermediate product that arises from the production of vinegar, there is a cloak of silence. In Iran there is a saying: 'Under the Shah, we drank openly and prayed in secret – nowadays it's the other way round!'

HERBS (Sabzi)
Fresh herbs are a very important component of the meal in Iran. The little herb basket is an integral part of the set table, and contains a variety of fresh herbs such as flat-leaf parsley, green coriander, chives, basil, and mint, as well as the tender leaves of radishes and the radishes themselves. Fresh herbs are sold everywhere in fairly large bundles, with the coarse stalks always being weighed with the leaves at the time of purchase. These stalks should always be removed before use.

For the recipes in this book, the gross weight at purchase is given: as a rule of thumb, once the herbs have been washed, trimmed and chopped, you will be left with a quantity of a little over half the weight of the original bunch. For many Persian dishes there are dried herb mixtures; if using these, reckon on about one-quarter of the gross weight of the fresh herbs. Many fresh herbs are available from ethnic shops, and also from mainstream grocers, who offer the more common herbs, usually with the coarse stems and roots already discarded.

KASHK AND OTHER DAIRY PRODUCTS
Medicinal value: cold and damp.

The basis of every Persian cheese (*panir*) is the souring of milk (*shir*) into yogurt (*mast*). In only a few areas of the north – among them, the Talesh region in the Alborz mountains – is cheese produced directly from milk. Elsewhere, milk is always first fermented to make yogurt, from which cheese can then be made in one of two ways: either the lactic-acid bacteria contained in the yogurt continue to ferment in a controlled fashion, or an enzyme is added to the yogurt that causes the milk protein to curdle. In Europe as well as Iran, rennet, an extract from the stomach, or abomasum, of an unweaned lamb, kid or calf, is used as a coagulant. In antiquity, other coagulants were also used, such as the whitish juice of the fig tree. Rennet cheese is of less importance in Iran, however, being popular only in Gilan.

Much more important, and ubiquitous in Persian cooking, is pure lactic-acid cheese and its derivatives: from milk that has undergone a controlled fermentation (yogurt) the fat is usually first removed. There are many ways of doing this, all practised in the different regions since ancient times. The yogurt is shaken and beaten in prepared goat- or cow-skins, pounded in wooden vessels, or shaken and whisked in clay amphorae. Since the 1970s, small, hand-operated centrifuges that work very effectively have also been used. In any case, the shaking, beating, pounding or whisking causes the cream, and finally the butter (*kareh*) to

collect. The butter is either used fresh for cooking, or heated and made into clarified butter which is ideal for cooking and frying, and was once the only fat used for either.

The liquid left over from the churning process – the buttermilk (*dugh*) – is usually drunk diluted with water, or it is further fermented, salted and boiled, until it yields a thickish, low-fat raw cheese. This raw cheese is now once again separated. In addition, it is hung in a very fine fabric sieve over a bowl. The semi-dry cheese curd (*shureh*, literally 'salt marsh') remains in the fabric, while the whey (*ab-e kashk*) collects in the bowl. The *shureh* is either eaten fresh, or made into little balls and dried further in the sun. The dried, hard balls are called *kashk*. The cheese will keep for years in this form, and is pounded and dissolved in water before further use.

Kashk is available from shops nowadays in two forms: in its original dried form as little balls, or in a jar, already dissolved in water and creamy. For the recipes in this book, *kashk* is used from the jar. It tastes strongly of ewe's or goat's milk, and needs to be boiled before consumption. It is then often used as a seasoning, or, mixed with water, as a sauce to accompany many stews and other dishes (*see* Tip on *Ash-e Reshteh*, page 60).

The whey that collects when *kashk* is made is either fed to the animals, or boiled once more and drained. What remains then is a brownish mass (*tarf*), which can still be used as a seasoning, but is no longer particularly prized. *Kashk* can be made with either ewe's, goat's, cow's or buffalo milk.

Camel's milk, on the other hand, although important to Turkish and Mongolian nomadic tribes, can be made into yogurt but is not suitable for making butter, for which a mixture of sheep's and goat's, or cow's and buffalo milk is generally used.

LENTILS (*Adas* and *Lapeh*)
Medicinal value: cold and dry.

With lentils, a basic distinction must be drawn between varieties that quickly cook down to a mush, and those that keep their 'bite'. Quick-cooking types, for example red or brown lentils, are good for dishes such as *ash*. Varieties that keep their 'bite' (e.g. black caviar lentils or green Puy lentils) are suitable for dishes like *Halim bademjan* or *Adas polo*.

The frequently used *lapeh*, often referred to as 'yellow' lentils, are available in any Asian grocer under the name of *chana dahl*. They are actually not lentils at all, but small, yellow, dehulled and split chickpeas, about the same size as yellow lentils, but thicker and above all requiring a considerably longer cooking time. Once they have soaked overnight, they must still be precooked for an additional 20–30 minutes for many dishes (this stage can also be handled in a pressure cooker).

Dried pulses should always be thoroughly washed in a bowl of water before use. Discard any loose debris that floats to the top.

LIMES (*Limu, Limu torsh*)
Medicinal value: cold and dry in the third degree.

The lime's juice is similar to that of the lemon, but stronger. Fresh limes are very juicy, and are ideal in *ablimu* (fresh lemonade or limeade).

Dried limes (*Limu omani*) shrink to the size and weight of a table-tennis ball, and are a useful addition to your store cupboard. Before they are cooked, they should be cut in half and deseeded, or pricked a couple of times and added to *khoresh* and *abgusht* dishes, which are given greater fragrance by this tart component. The cooked limes in *khoresh* can be eaten, peel and all. Some find their taste too intense, while others consider them particularly delicate. Fresh limes are widely available; dried limes are available at Persian grocery stores.

MINT (*Nana*)
Medicinal value: warm.

Nana-mint or spearmint is usually available dried in central Europe. Even when dried, it still retains its unmistakeable, delicious flavour. Dried mint can be bought at any grocer's, finely chopped and ready for use. When using it for cooking, rub it to a powder between your fingers to release the flavourful oils. Dried, whole spearmint leaves are also ideal for brewing into tea. The taste, reminiscent of peppermint tea, has its own, very refined note.

Clockwise from top left: Dried rose petals at the bazaar; barberries; an onion field; saffron.

MULBERRIES (Tut)
Medicinal value: cold when unripe; warm when ripe or dried.

Mulberries are eaten fresh, or served dried as a sweet snack. Their dried taste is reminiscent of that of choice raisins. The mulberry tree also plays a role in silk production: its leaves are the staple food of the silkworm.

NOODLES (Reshteh)

Noodles are native to eastern Asia, and Marco Polo is said to have brought them back from China to Venice. They seem to have left remarkably few traces behind on the return journey, however. In Persian cooking they have a very limited place, occurring more or less only in particular *ash* recipes (*see recipe for Ash-e Reshteh*). *Ash* noodles are a wholly distinct variety of noodle for which there is no real substitute. A similar result can only be achieved with Japanese Udon noodles, available from more adventurous supermarkets and from Asian shops.

OKRA (Bamieh)
Medicinal value: cold and very damp; meant to subdue a hot-blooded temperament.

Originally from Africa, okra was first introduced in Iran by the Arabs in the 19th century, and is now grown and eaten primarily in Azerbaijan and Kurdistan. Even today, many Persians are not particularly fond of this vegetable, as careless handling can result in a sauce with an unappetizingly viscous consistency. Preparing okra requires a degree of flair, as the hard stalk end needs to be trimmed without damaging the pod itself. Buy only tender young pods, which should be cooked whole. Stir the pods carefully and take care not to cook them over too fierce a heat, so that they do not burst!

PEPPER (Felfel)
Medicinal value: dry and warm in the fourth degree.

When black peppercorns are harvested unripe, the dried berries are peeled to produce white pepper. Black pepper is a frequent, popular addition to Persian cooking – unlike the South American native fruits of the capsicum family such as chillies, cayenne peppers and sweet peppers, which are often also referred to as peppers (or *peperoni* in Italian).

These vegetables (or the chilli powder and paprika made from them) are only infrequently used in Persian cuisine, in such dishes as *Dolmeh felfel* (stuffed peppers), *Torshi felfel sabz* (pickled hot peppers), and *Khorak-e lubia sabz* (braised meat with green beans).

PISTACHIOS (Pesteh)
Medicinal value: warm in the second degree.

The most outstanding Persian delicacy of them all is the pistachio, once served to the ancient kings of Persia. Today, Iran is the world's largest exporter of pistachios, yet even in Iran itself, good pistachios are expensive.

Available plain, slightly salted or given a tart twist with a squeeze of lemon juice, the most famous varieties are *pesteh akbari* and *pesteh kalleh quchi*. Iranians are fond of describing pistachios, once known as *akbari*, as 'Akbar's pistachios', a reference to the Iranian ex-president Akbar Rafsanjani, one of the country's biggest plantation owners. Only dried pistachios are suitable to export, as, when fresh, the nuts have a downy shell and a delicate taste but do not keep very long. Used in both sweet and savoury dishes, pistachios are eaten primarily as a snack.

POMEGRANATE (Anar)
Medicinal value: cold and dry.

The pomegranate is known to have been used as a burial object in ancient Egypt, and is also often portrayed on old Persian rugs. The ripe fruit of the pomegranate tree contains a cluster of closely packed, sweetly acidic red seeds or kernels, separated by light-coloured membranes. When the fruit is fully ripened and fresh (with a shiny, plump skin), these kernels are very juicy. Delicious pomegranate juice can be squeezed from such fruit, either by putting it through a juice press, or simply by rolling it on a countertop with your hand, then piercing a small hole in the side of the fruit and squeezing hard.

To get to the seeds easily, cut off the 'crown' of the fruit and lightly score the outer skin from top to bottom about six times. Then put the fruit into a bowl of water and leave for 5 minutes. Holding the cut fruit under the water, to prevent being spattered by the juice, which stains, remove the outer peel so that the inner white membrane is visible, then gently tear the sections apart. The plump seeds can now be removed easily; discard the peel and membranes. Eat the seeds raw and plain, or, according to taste, with a little salt or sugar sprinkled on top.

POMEGRANATE SYRUP (Robb-e anar)

Pomegranate syrup is available in small bottles in Persian grocers. The quality of the industrially produced syrup, however, is usually substantially lower than that of freshly squeezed pomegranate juice thickened by boiling. When you have the chance to buy fresh, juicy pomegranates at the market, you should seize the opportunity and make the syrup yourself. To do this, squeeze the juice from the pomegranates and boil it with a little salt for between 1 and 2 hours in an uncovered pan over a moderate heat until thickened, stirring occasionally. Depending on the variety of pomegranate, the juice, and consequently the syrup, will be sweet, sweet-sour, or sour. The colour of the syrup also depends on the type of pomegranate used. In Iran, pomegranate syrup is either manufactured industrially, or produced domestically or artisanally in a traditional fashion. Homemade production, for example, can be seen in areas around the city of Saveh, northwest of Tehran (near the city of Qazvin on the road to Hamadan), where there are extensive pomegranate plantations. In the autumn, housewives busy themselves producing the syrup, which is then exported in large quantities to other cities.

Stored in a cool place, pomegranate syrup will keep for several months.

RICE (Berenj)

The Persian language has many words for rice: raw, it is called *berenj*; cooked (depending on how it is prepared), it becomes *chelo* or *kateh*; and combined with other ingredients it is known as *polo*. There are countless varieties of rice, each with their own names. Rice is the focal point of Persian cuisine, elevated to this position by the chefs of the Safavid court. Originally from China or India, basmati rice was traded very early on – even the ancient Romans were familiar with it, although rice was still very expensive at the time of Roman Empire, and was used more as a medicine than a food. Persian rice is always hulled (basmati) rice. The essential criteria when buying are that it be white, long-grained, and fragrant.

Anyone wishing to cook Persian rice should really go to a Iranian or Afghan trader and ask him to recommend a particular variety of rice. The rice sold by European grocers is usually only a pale imitation of the genuine Persian article. Preparing Persian rice successfully is a true art, and depends on a number of factors: the variety and age of the rice, the cooker, and the pan. With a little practice and patience, anyone can cook perfect Persian rice, and preparation is described in detail in the recipes section. Perfectly cooked rice is fluffy and dry, with long, tender grains that remain completely intact.

ROSES (Gol)

Medicinal value: warm; good for the nerves and heart, and for kidney and stomach complaints.

Roses have been used and grown for many centuries in the Mediterranean and Asia, for aesthetic, medicinal, and culinary purposes. Ancient Egyptians used roses as burial objects, and the Greek island of Rhodes was named after them. *Rosa gallica, Rosa moschata,* and *Rosa damascena* are all famous scented roses.

The petals of particularly fragrant varieties are also used in rose jam (*morabba-ye gol, gol-qand*). Dried rose petals are available from Persian shops. They should be rubbed to a powder between the fingers when used in such dishes as *Chaloqmeh* (Safavid-style savoury pastries), or added to yogurt or *dugh* (*see* Recipes).

ROSE-WATER (Golab)

The distillation of rose-water from the petals of roses was noted by Avicenna in the 11th century. The rose-water from Kashan is particularly famous. Every year in the Persian month of *Ordibehesht* (April/May), thousands of tourists flock to this city to take part in the rose-picking and distilling ceremonies. The petals of the Damascene rose are picked in the early morning, when their scent is at its most intense. They are then sorted in a cool room and distilled with water in a large iron pan according to the traditional method. The distillate thus obtained is the rose-water. Nowadays other techniques are also sometimes used, and special solvents exist that can lengthen the life of the ingredients.

Rose-water is used to enhance a number of desserts, and is also often sprayed in mosques for its scent. Men use it to groom their beards, and women as a mild facial toner. Rose oil is a very strong extract from rose-water. Four tonnes of rose petals are needed to produce a litre (35fl oz) of rose oil, and this is reflected in the correspondingly astronomical price.

SAFFRON (Zafaran)

Medicinal value: warm in the third degree.

Obtained from the stigma of the saffron crocus, saffron originated in Greece, probably on the island of Crete, but has been spread through trade in the Mediterranean and Asia since the earliest times. Today, about 80 per cent of the world's saffron crop is grown in Iran and Spain. About 150,000 crocus flowers are needed to produce 1 kg (2¼ lb) dried saffron. Genuine Persian saffron is indispensable for true Persian cuisine, and it does not come cheap. Do not be tempted to buy ready-ground saffron.

The risk of buying an inferior imitation is particularly high with the powder, and even when you actually manage to find the genuine article, ground saffron loses its flavour very quickly. Reliable vendors will only sell saffron threads, and although expensive, they are worth every penny. It is impossible to produce genuine saffron on the cheap. The threads should be very finely ground with a good pinch of sugar in a small mortar (or in a small teacup with the blunt handle of a knife) just before use. Depending on the recipe, the ground saffron can then be dissolved in a little hot water before use. A little genuine Persian saffron goes a very long way, imparting a fine, unmistakeable flavour to foods.

SUGAR (Shekar), ROCK SUGAR (Qand)
Medicinal value: warm in the fourth degree.

Sugar can be obtained from a variety of plants. Cane sugar was introduced to Europe in the early Middle Ages by Arab merchants, who had obtained it from Persian traders, who in turn had been introduced to the sweetener by the Indians. The Sanskrit *sharkara* actually means 'gravel', and this term was applied to sugar in its crystalline form. The term *sharkara* was not only used to denote cane sugar, however, but also to sugar derived from other plant sources. The sugar of antiquity (*sakharon* in ancient Greek), which originated in India but also spread via Persian trade, was the secretion of certain types of bamboo, and was given the figurative Persian name of *tabashir* (literally, 'chalk' or 'magnesium carbonate'). The Sanskrit *sharkara* gave rise to the Persian *shakar*, rendered in Arabic as *sukar*, from which the terms for sugar in the various European languages eventually evolved.

Nowadays, normal white or brown sugar is referred to as *shekar*, while *qand* denotes the solid, crystalline rock sugar, bits of which are broken off and taken with tea, or the solid sugar hewn from large blocks. Small pieces of the latter are laid directly on the tongue (it melts less quickly than sugar cubes eaten in the West) to flavour hot tea as it is drunk.

SUMAC (Somaq)
Medicinal value: antiseptic in effect.

The dried, ground rust-red fruit of the sumac tree — also known as the vinegar tree on account of the astringent tang of its fruit — has an assertive note in its taste, and therefore needs to be used with care. Sumac very seldom blends well with delicately fragrant spices such as saffron. It is used primarily in *kabab* dishes.

TAMARIND (Tamr-e hendi)
Medicinal value: contains a complex volatile oil; has an antiseptic, antipyretic effect; promotes digestion.

The tamarind, a large, bean-shaped capsule with a tart, tangy taste, comes from east Africa. The Arabs named it *tamar hindi*, 'Indian date (palm)', on account of the fruit's brown pulp, although the tree is neither a palm, nor did it originate in India. The fruit is usually sold pressed into blocks, which must then be dissolved in a little water; it is also available in jars as a paste. Tamarind is used as an acidulant in soups and fish dishes.

TURMERIC (Zardchubeh)
Medicinal value: warm in the first degree. Effective against inflammations and offers protection to the liver; stimulates digestion and circulation.

Since earliest times, turmeric has been viewed as a less-expensive substitute for saffron. The only thing that turmeric has in common with saffron, however, is that it colours food most effectively, imparting a yellow, rather than a reddish tinge. Otherwise, it is different in every respect: saffron is obtained from the stigma of a crocus, while turmeric comes from the rhizome of the turmeric plant, which belongs to the *Zingiberaceae* (ginger) family. Nor do the two plants have much in common in terms of taste. Ground turmeric is a popular addition to Persian cooking, often used with fried onions or to season meat. It is nearly always sautéed briefly with the other ingredients, which causes it to lose its slightly bitter taste.

Right: Bolbol, the Persian nightingale, was extolled by Hafez, and plays a central role in Persian poetry.

WALNUTS (Gerdu)
Medicinal value: warm.

One of the best-known Persian recipes featuring walnuts is *Khoresht-e fesenjan* (Duck with walnuts). For walnuts that taste fresh from the tree, remove the shells and scald the nutmeats in boiling water; add a little salt, and soak until the water goes cold. With a fruit knife, it will now be easy to free the kernels from the thin, slightly bitter surrounding membrane. Served with sheep cheese, fresh flatbread and some seedless green grapes, walnuts make a delicious little appetizer.

WINE (Sharab)
see GRAPES

YOGURT: DRINKING (Dugh)
Medicinal value: cold and damp.

Dugh is a spicy drink made of yogurt and water, slightly salted and seasoned with dried mint or other herbs, such as *puneh* (wild marjoram). Dugh is served chilled as a refreshing drink and to accompany meals.

GLOSSARY

PERSIAN–ENGLISH

ab	water	*geshniz*	coriander
ab-e ghureh	verjuice (the juice of unripe grapes)	*ghureh*	unripe grapes
ab-e kashk	whey	*gol*	rose
ab-e miveh	freshly squeezed fruit juice	*golab*	rose-water
abgusht	meat broth with pounded meat	*golabi*	pear
ablimu	lemon juice, lime juice	*gol-kalam*	cauliflower
adas	lentils	*gosfand*	mutton, sheep
adasi	lentil dip	*gusht*	meat
al(u)balu	sour cherries	*halal*	allowed (according to Muslim dietary laws)
alu	plums, mirabelles, yellow prunes		
anar	pomegranate	*haram*	forbidden
anbeh	mango	*havij*	carrot
angur	grapes	*hel*	cardamom
ash	thick soup	*hendevaneh*	watermelon
ash-pazi	kitchen, cooking, cuisine	*holu*	peach
ba	with	*ja'fari*	parsley
badam	almonds	*jo*	barley
bademjan	aubergine	*jujeh*	poussin
bamieh	okra	*juz*	nut, nutmeg
baqala, baqali	broad (fava) beans, jack beans	*kadu*	squash, pumpkin, courgette (zucchini)
barg	leaf		
barg-e mou	vine leaves	*kakuti; avishan-e shirazi*	wild thyme, creeping thyme
beh	quince	*kebab*	grilled or pan-fried meat
berenj	rice (raw)	*kalam*	cabbage
beryani	grilled or pan-fried dish	*kalam-pich*	white cabbage, savoy (curly) cabbage
borani	vegetable dish with yogurt		
boz	billygoat, goat	*karafs*	celery
chay	tea	*kareh*	butter
chelo	fluffy white rice cooked in two stages, without additional ingredients	*kashk*	dried *shureh*
		kateh	a relatively compact white rice, cooked in a single stage
choghondar	turnip, root vegetable	*keshmesh*	raisins
choghondar-e labu'i	beetroot	*kharboze*	melon
daneh	seed, grain	*khaviar*	caviar
darchin	cinnamon	*khiar*	cucumber
dast	hand	*khoda*	God
dig	kettle, pot	*khorak*	food, fare, rations; goulash
dolmeh	stuffed vegetables	*khoresh(t)*	ragout, stew
dugh	yogurt drink	*khorma*	dates
-e	(links a noun with an adjective)	*kot(e)let*	rissole, patty
esfenaj	spinach	*kubideh*	pounded
felfel	pepper, paprika, sweet pepper	*kufteh*	meatballs
garm	warm	*kuku*	omelet
gav	ox, steer	*lapeh*	yellow lentils (hulled, split chickpeas)
gerdu	walnut		

limu	lime	*sarshir*	cream
limu omani	dried lime	*sefid*	white
lubia	green beans, French beans	*shahr*	city
mah	month	*shanbalile*	fenugreek
mahi	fish	*sharab*	wine
mahicheh	calf (of leg), muscle, leg	*sharbat*	(thickened) fruit juice
mast	yogurt	*shekar*	sugar
mehman	guest	*shir*	milk
miveh	fruit	*shirin*	sweet
mixak	cloves	*shureh*	semi-dried cheese curd from
morabba	jam		fermented and salted buttermilk
morgh	chicken	*sib*	apple
mo	grapevine	*sibzamin*	potato
mouz	banana	*sir*	garlic
musir	wild garlic	*siyah*	black
namak	salt	*somaq*	sumac
nan	bread	*sorkh*	red
na'na	mint	*ta'arof*	courtesy ritual
naranj	bitter orange	*tabeh*	pan, frying pan
no	new	*tah*	base
noruz	New Year	*tahdig*	rice crust
nokhodchi	chickpeas	*tamr*	date
nokhod-sabz	green peas	*tamr-e hendi*	tamarind
paludeh	sweet fruit juice drink	*tarf*	whey extract
panir	cheese	*torshi*	vegetables pickled in vinegar
pesteh	pistachios	*tokhm-e morgh*	hen's egg
piaz	onion	*tut*	mulberries
polo	fluffy white rice cooked in two	*va*	and
	stages and mixed with other	*ya*	or
	ingredients	*zaban*	tongue
portoqal	orange	*za'faran*	saffron
puneh	wild marjoram, true oregano	*zamin*	earth, soil
qahve	coffee	*zard*	yellow, golden
qand	rock sugar	*zardchubeh*	turmeric
qeymeh	minced (ground) meat, very finely	*zereshk*	barberry, buckthorn
	sliced meat	*zeytun*	olives
reshteh	noodles	*zireh*	cumin
rivas	rhubarb		
robb-e anar	pomegranate syrup		
roughan	clarified butter; oil		
sabz	green		
sabzi	greens, herbs, vegetables		
sadeh	simple, clear		
salad	salad		
sard	cold		

INDEX

The Publishers extend their cordial thanks to Ms Heidrun Niemann, who placed valuable antiques from her shop *Caravanserai* in Munich at our disposal for the photography; to the restaurant *Pars*, which let us into its kitchens; to that treasure trove of pretty accessories, Ali Baba, which was kind enough to lend us original crockery from Iran; and to Ms Mahin Atrafe, who helped with the cooking.